"Dawn's timely message about our addiction to approval and the desperate need to fight for recovery prompts us to approach our insecurities with honesty and courage and discover joy in the surrendered life God intended for us."

—**Angie Smith**, women's ministry speaker and
best-selling author of *I Will Carry You* and *Mended*

"Dawn has written a powerful book that every woman needs to read! We miss so much of our God-given purposes in fear of what other flawed humans think. Thank you, Dawn, for bravely sharing with us the solution to these oft-challenging fears and feelings: a deeper trust in the God who made us."

—**Lara Casey**, author of *Make it Happen* and *Cultivate*

"We've all felt the allure of social approval and the disappointment of an online post or real-life relationship falling flat. *Like Me or Not* shows us a different way as Dawn's practical tips and vulnerable stories call us to greater levels of freedom in Christ."

—**Jen Weaver**, author of *A Wife's Secret to Happiness*

"*Like Me or Not* was a liberating read for me as a woman. I believe this book is going to empower women everywhere to start seeing themselves a little more like God sees us."

—**Laura L. Bento**, CEO, *Good Grit Magazine*

"*Like Me or Not* is a helpful guide for those who struggle with people-pleasing. Dawn, with surprising candor, takes the rea̶d̶e̶r̶ ̶t̶h̶r̶o̶u̶g̶h̶ ̶h̶e̶r̶ own journey, and offers tangible ste̶p̶ and perfectionism are part of your n̶ for you."

—**Lucille Zimmern̶** ̶o̶r̶ *Renewed*

"*Like Me or Not* gives thoughtful, biblical, practical help for all of us who seek the approval of others. It is truly a crucial book for the twenty-first century."

—**Bob Hostetler**, coauthor with Josh McDowell of
Don't Check Your Brains at the Door

"*Like Me or Not* allowed me to feel more confident in my decisions and completely surrender to God's will instead of the opinions of others. If you're constantly seeking approval, this is the book for you."

—**Bethany Jett**, award-winning author of *The Cinderella Rule: A Young Woman's Guide to Happily Ever After.*

"*Like Me or Not* is inspiring and uplifting. We all require tools to navigate the storms of people-pleasing. This is a must read on the path to self-discovery!"

—**Meghan Noone**, model/spokesperson, Executive Director, Noonetime Charities

"Dawn has opened the door of her life to connect with countless people who share her same addiction. *Like Me or Not* serves as a practical resource to bring healing to the approval addict. This authentic approach to new life is a journey worth taking."

—**Micah Andrews**, CEO, Foundry Ministries

"Dawn's book is a must-read for all women. I'm grateful that God prompted Dawn to write such an honest and powerful book."

—**Michelle Medlock Adams**, best-selling author of more than eighty books

"Dawn addresses this important topic in an honest, personable, and loving way. For too long the standards by which we judge ourselves have been unreasonable and downright false. Dawn not only addresses the problem of approval addiction, she offers a Christ-centered, practical strategy to solve it."

—**Dr. Janet L. McMullen**, Associate Professor of Communications, University of North Alabama

Like Me Or Not

OVERCOMING APPROVAL ADDICTION

DAWN M. OWENS

WORTHY®
PUBLISHING

To Bob Hostetler—

What you hold in your hands
is the product of your spiritual legacy.

This "Ehud" is forever grateful.

Contents

. . . .

INTRODUCTION

Could I Have a Problem?

• • • • • • • • • •

Before you can break out of prison, you first
must realize you are locked up.

HEALTHYPLACE.COM

Jessica knew there were some underlying issues in her life. She could feel it, especially when she was around Kayla, who just seemed to have it all together. She couldn't put her finger on why, but every conversation she had with Kayla felt like a fierce competition. Sometimes it was what their kids were (or were not) doing. Other times, it was who had gotten the better bargain or whose husband was doing more around the house. Every time they talked, Jessica felt compelled to outdo Kayla in some way. She even found herself wondering at times what Kayla was doing and whether she should be doing the same thing.

Social media didn't help. Kayla would post updates, and people would respond and engage her in the comments. People often liked her comments or her posts, and the pictures of her kids got likes and comments about how cute or precious they were or how big they were getting. Jessica's posts got attention too, but every time she checked, Kayla's page had more comments, likes, and shares than Jessica's—even though they shared many of the same friends and followers. What was Kayla doing differently—or better—than Jessica? Why did people seem to care so much more about Kayla's life? Why couldn't Jessica reproduce Kayla's following?

Tanya, on the other hand, found herself exhausted at the end of most weeks. She couldn't figure out why she never seemed to get anything on her to-do list accomplished; she felt like she was always doing things for everyone else. It's not that she didn't want to do things for others—she knew that in doing so she was being like Jesus, and she wanted to be more like Jesus—but it was exhausting her. There had to be a way out. Besides, her boss was getting on her at work. He'd even accused her of being more concerned with what everyone else was doing than with her own workload. Didn't he see how she got her stuff done too (just not always on his timeline)? Tanya felt angry at her boss for insinuating that she didn't care about her work. Maybe if he would just do his job and quit asking her for things all the time, it would help her to concentrate on her own work.

And then there's Rachel—midtwenties, pretty, single, and ready to be in a God-centered relationship. She knew she wanted a man who would be just as in love with Jesus as she was, but she couldn't seem to find him. Afraid she'd miss an opportunity to meet Mr. Right, Rachel went out with any guy who asked her. To avoid rejection, she even sometimes compromised her standards, something she had promised God she would not do.

Each of these women was addicted to approval. Approval addiction can shortchange relationships, cause turmoil in families, erode friendships, and break down marriages. Jessica didn't realize the reason she felt like she was in competition with Kayla was because her high need for approval made her feel inadequate. Tanya was so wrapped up in seeking approval from others that she forgot to seek God's approval, so most of the time, she just wound up angry. And Rachel's fear of rejection caused her to compromise her values, and that left her feeling empty and lonely. These women are vivid examples of how an approval addiction can modify your decisions and behaviors and result in the very things you most want to avoid.

Did anything in these stories echo situations or conversations in your life? Did you find yourself empathizing with any of the women? You might not be ready to say, "Yes, I have an addiction to approval," but you know there's something there. Let me offer some questions that may help you decide.

- Are you preoccupied with what other people think about you?
- Is it difficult for you to know what you want?
- Do you find yourself saying yes when you desperately want to say no?
- Is it hard for you to express your feelings when they differ from the opinions of people you are close to?
- Does your happiness depend on the approval of others?[1]

If you answered at least one of these questions affirmatively, you have a need for approval. If you answered yes to all of them, you may have a full-blown addiction. Either way, there is great hope. Step one in overcoming your addiction is recognizing you have a problem; step two is getting help. You are in the right place.

You Are Not Alone

I am here to walk with you and encourage you, from Chapter 1 all the way to the end. Jessica, Tanya, and Rachel are all parts of my addiction. There is no area touched on in this book that I haven't personally dealt with on some level. I've often wondered if God allowed me to experience so many of these symptoms of addiction so I could write this book for others to learn from and experience true healing.

This book will help you identify how your addiction to approval manifests itself in your life. It is not a how-to guide; rather, it will present an ongoing process that you can work through regularly and repetitively. You must be willing to fight for your recovery by seeking God on a daily basis. Sometimes you'll feel like you've conquered one area . . . only to find out you've messed up again in another. Thankfully, your Savior offers you grace in the times you need it most.

Some chapters of this book may speak specifically into your current situation, while others may not track with where you are right now. That's okay. Work on where you are. Allow God to speak to you in one area for a while and then, when you've arrived at a healthier place, return to the book to work on another.

No matter how it works for you, I pray that over time, you will experience healing from this debilitating addiction. You don't have to live in bondage; hope is not lost.

Every Alcoholics Anonymous, Narcotics Anonymous, and Celebrate Recovery meeting ends the same way—with the group holding hands and reciting a prayer. I can't think of a better way to end this introduction to our journey together. Imagine all of us approval addicts in a room together, realizing we are at the beginning of something great. We've experienced the first meeting and are ready to take on tomorrow, whatever it may bring. Let's join hands in our hearts and minds and recite the Lord's Prayer together:

Our Father which art in heaven, hallowed be thy name. Thy kingdom come, thy will be done in earth, as it is in heaven. Give us this day our daily bread. And forgive us our debts, as we forgive our debtors. And lead us not into temptation, but deliver us from evil: for thine is the kingdom, and the power, and the glory, for ever. Amen.[2]

Reality Check

* * * * * * * * * *

It's in Christ that we find out who we are
and what we are living for.

EPHESIANS 1:11 MSG

Hi. My name is Dawn Owens, and I am an approval addict. To make it even worse, I have a severe attachment to finding my approval through social media. Just last week, I found myself comparing a recent post with past posts to see if the number of likes I'd received had increased.

It's true.

Writing a book on how to overcome the addiction to approval might be the most difficult way to break that addiction. Seriously, do you know how many people must approve of your idea before your book is published?

The reality is, popularity sells, so . . . why in the world would a recovering approval addict choose to go through a deliberate process of seeking people's approval when there may be only a miniscule chance of success in it? This seems a lot like an alcoholic hanging out at her favorite bar.

The answer is simple: *you.*

You are the reason why I, a recovering approval addict, would write a book about how to overcome the addiction to approval. "But we don't even know each other," you say. That may be true. However, I'll bet I know some things about you.

First, you picked up this book because you or someone you know (wink, wink) is addicted to approval. Let's be real. *You* have an addiction to approval. You know it; I know it; and now the person who checked you out at the bookstore or fulfilled your Amazon order probably knows it too. In fact, you might even have thought about *not* purchasing this book for fear of what the cashier would think about you. Maybe you've even strategized placing this book some-where inconspicuous, so your friends don't see you reading a book about overcoming an addiction to approval. Or maybe you are even sneakier than I imagine, and you saw the book at the bookstore but decided this one was a good e-read—no one will ever know what you struggle with since it's only on your e-book device. Smooth.

Next, you're wondering if it's possible to overcome an addiction to craving people's approval. Well, I can tell you, you *can* overcome it. But don't misunderstand the word *overcome*, which means "to get the better of in a struggle or conflict; conquer; defeat."[3] You will not overcome this addiction without a struggle. But the definition also indicates it's a successful struggle. We can say amen to that. If I'm go-ing to struggle with something, of course I want it to end successfully!

You're probably also wondering whether you're the only one you know who struggles with an approval addiction. I know I did, until I started telling people I was writing a book on the topic. Then a floodgate opened. It became a normal conversation for me:

"I hear you're writing a book. What's it called?"

"Well, the working title is, *Like Me or Not: Overcoming the Addiction to Approval.*"

"Oh . . . I need to read that book. Is it based on liking people's statuses online? Because, yeah, that is totally an issue. And it's amazing how addicted you can become to wanting people's approval—and not just online."

And if I happened to be in a group when the question was asked, suddenly everyone would sound off, sharing stories about themselves or people they knew who ached for approval and how social media feeds into the addiction.

So be assured—you are not alone. There is hardly a human being, male or female, on Planet Earth who does not struggle with the need for approval to some degree. Well, let me clarify: most of us are addicted to approval, but not everyone knows it. Most are addicted, but not everyone struggles to overcome. To some it is bothersome, like a cowlick that refuses to be combed flat, but to others, it is a full-blown addiction, and they are desperately in need of help. Regardless of which camp you land in, this book can bring a measure of hope.

The last thing I think I know about you is that you are ready to get some help. How do I know this? Well, you picked up the book, right? And you've read this far and have yet to put it down. This is a good place to be. Here you can find redemption, grace, freedom, and healing. After all, you can't break free of something if you don't know you're in bondage to it. I know this is true because I have been in your shoes and have walked the path before you. I have struggled with every symptom in this book—and then some.

In my struggles, I have learned about an amazing God who offers me redemption from my past and the negative choices I've made in my need for approval. At times, I have faltered and believed old lies, and I've allowed those lies to lead to unhealthy choices. Thankfully, God has taught me how to break free and make new choices. Through this process, I have received healing.

An approval addict's wounds go deep and can be slow to heal because of the number of times we scratch them open. For many, the wounds have left scars we don't want others to see. But scars fade and even disappear in the light of the wonderful gift Jesus gave us when He decided to choose the approval of God over the approval of man. When we do the same, our scars become so insignificant to us that we no longer realize they are there.

With that in mind, we overcome our addiction to approval by the blood, sweat, and tears Jesus shed on the cross. It's my prayer that you will come to define success only by the things God says in His Word are true of you. I also pray that your need for the approval of others will steadily decrease, even as your need for and reliance upon God increases.

Let's Get Real

Now that you know I am a recovering approval addict, it's also important to know I have been ministering to drug and alcohol addicts for years. As the founder and executive director of The Link of Cullman County, Inc., a faith-based nonprofit agency working to break the cycle of poverty, I constantly face the realities and challenges of addiction and recovery.

I have seen people win in their struggle for sobriety, and I have wept with an aching and broken heart over the loss associated with addiction. An approval addict may not be pumping her veins full of heroin, but the addiction still claims casualties. It destroys confidence and self-esteem. It destroys lives. People have chosen suicide rather than the continued struggle of living up to the expectations of others.

There are, in fact, some who have been caught up in substance abuse *because* they were unable to identify and address the root cause of their struggles—the need for approval. Addiction is layered and complex, but we can take comfort and hope in knowing that there is a God who can overcome it all.

Of course, this book will only be as beneficial as you make it. Each chapter will help you understand another facet of what causes your need for approval and then provide Scripture for you to use to renew your mind and eventually transform your actions. I love the New Living Translation's version of Romans 12:2: "Don't copy the behavior and customs of this world, but let God transform you into a new person by changing the way you think. Then you will learn to know God's will for you, which is good and pleasing and perfect."

So much of our need for others' approval comes because we have believed the lie that we must copy the behaviors and customs of this world to be accepted. Consequently, we respond to social media in ways deemed acceptable by our social circles, we wear clothes because of the trends around us, and we decorate our homes to reflect the latest and greatest HGTV show. We can look all around us and see ways in which we have conformed to this world.

The good news is that we can live in the world without conforming to it when we allow God to transform our lives. By renewing our minds through the Bible, we can know what God's good and perfect will is for us; we'll no longer worry about what other people think or expect. I don't know about you, but I take comfort in that idea. For years, I felt like I was constantly striving to live up to someone else's expectations; I desperately craved their approval. Now I know who I am and, most days, the only one I seek to please is God. And I have gained this freedom only by renewing my mind with His Word.

As a recovering approval addict, I am still tempted every day to seek approval from some other source than God, but things are different now. Before, I would have landed in a never-ending spiral of negative thoughts; I'd have distanced myself from others, blamed the culprit, become a victim, felt shame and guilt, and ultimately, I'd have distanced myself from God. Now I am equipped with the tools to combat those thoughts. I am equipped with God's Word, and I've learned that all I need to do is trust and obey Him. Obedience provides freedom and blessing that only He can give. Because of Him, I am free from the need to perform for others.

Writing this book has been a humbling experience. There are so many sets of eyes on every word I write, analyzing each story from my life. Even the thought of you reading this book makes me feel vulnerable and emotional. But this journey has become my sacrificial offering to the Lord. After all, these are His stories; this is the testimony He has created for my life.

It is my hope and prayer that, through my experience, the related truth of Scripture, and the Holy Spirit's help, you will identify your areas of struggle and experience deliverance. I'm right here with you, too. Picture me walking beside you throughout this journey, praying for you, believing in your healing, and offering you grace as you learn more of who you are and how much He loves you.

Let's commit together, today, to start praying for freedom—freedom from the bondage of jealousy, competition, division, self-centeredness, self-pity, self-doubt, neediness, and enslavement to other people's perceptions of us. To overcome our addictions, we must learn to focus less on ourselves and more on others. I'll commit to pray for you, and I invite you to pray for me and all the other women reading this book. Pray with me:

Lord Jesus, I recognize that I have a need for approval in my life, and I have sought to meet that need through other people rather than through You. Please forgive me for getting this mixed up. I did not realize that I was basing my decisions on other people's approval of me and not on Your desire for me. I submit this addiction to You right now. I ask You to begin the process of restoring me. Just as You cured the blind man, the leper, and the woman with the issue of blood, I ask You to heal me from this addiction. I realize the process may take a while, and I am willing to cooperate with Your Holy Spirit to receive the wisdom and discernment I need. Remind me to seek You daily in prayer and in Your Word. Help me also to find someone to whom I can be accountable as I walk this path. Amen.

2

Puhlease, People

· · · · · · · · · · ·

There is something very addictive about people-
pleasing. It's a thought pattern and a habit that feels
really, really good until it becomes desperate.

ANNE HATHAWAY

Confession time. I use Facebook, Twitter, Instagram, and other social media—and I like it. A lot. I use social media to share my life with friends near and far. I also use it to promote the goings-on of the ministry I serve. We desire to love the poor through encouragement, education, and employability training; in doing so we provide opportunity for life-transformational experiences with Jesus. We do this in the hope of alleviating the effects of poverty in homes throughout our community.

Throughout the year, we coach and encourage those who have been battling with addiction to walk in sobriety and learn who they are in Christ. We teach inmates how they can be set free in Jesus and reconciled with families, gain employment, and serve their community. We mentor children from economically challenged homes and difficult family situations to help them gain confidence in themselves and their academic abilities. We teach teenagers to become wise with their money so they can break the cycle of generational poverty. These are just a few of the examples of how God has used our ministry over the years.

Each year, we run an end-of-the-year fund-raising campaign. From October through December, we write letters, release video testimonials, and share stories on our social media channels. We ask the public to financially support life transformation. This time of year can be a lot of fun, but it is also challenging for a recovering approval addict like me.

Recently, a unique opportunity presented itself through a national grant program. To receive the grant, we had to recruit people from all over the United States to vote for our cause. We asked the grant organization for funds to help us create a safe place in our little community in North Alabama for foster children to feel supported, learn life skills, and discover who they are in Christ.

They read our proposal and selected us as one of two hundred causes to compete for the grant. Now, Cullman County's population is eighty-two thousand people, with a central city of fifteen thousand. Compared to the other locations that were selected—many of them large urban centers—we were an underdog hoping to see God do a miracle. We knew it was a David-and-Goliath opportunity, but when you are passionate about the people you serve, you do what you can to help your cause win, especially when twenty-five thousand dollars is at stake.

The grant-making organization posted the top two hundred causes online and asked people to select the final forty via daily online voting. Social media was crucial, of course. We used every method we could think of to get the word out. Our community does not have a large TV station, so Facebook Live became a critical tool for us. Facebook Live allows a user to go "live" via video to share whatever they are doing in real time. It is an incredible tool, but it can be extremely intimidating.

We decided to share stories of why foster care programs mattered so much to our community and why every single vote was so important. For ten days we rallied our supporters to vote. I felt like a local newscaster as I traveled around, interviewing people who were directly affected by the foster care crisis in our area. The community responded enthusiastically to this new area of our ministry.

But, as you know, I am a recovering approval addict, and though Facebook Live was fun to use, it was also trying for me. Every day, I was online and live in front of whoever might be watching. Some days, the crowd of watchers grew and commented and engaged with me. Other days, they fell a little silent. All kinds of folks logged on to watch. One of the most exciting moments for me was when the president of the Christian Community Development Association (CCDA), a national organization to which we belong, started following. He was in Chicago, and I felt like I'd hit the big time by gaining his attention.

All this video time meant that every morning, how I looked and what I was wearing was high priority. I woke a bit earlier to make sure my hair and makeup were perfect. I studied YouTube videos on how to do my makeup a certain way to make sure it looked good for the camera.

Once you are live, you can see how many people are watching you. If you are friends with them on Facebook, their names pop up for you to see. Anyone watching can leave comments and/or choose emoticons like a thumbs-up, a heart, a wow face, a sad face, or an angry face. They can communicate with you both during your live event and after. As you can imagine, this can be a tightrope walk for an approval addict like me, whose first impulse is to see all those who are watching as people to be pleased. The process challenged me to stay focused on pleasing only God and not seeking to please other people.

I have hosted Facebook Live events that many people attended and others that felt like I was all alone. Had this been years ago, I would have given up after my first event, overwhelmed by the fear of what people were thinking. Thankfully, I have learned I'm not here to please people; I'm here to seek the pleasure of God. But it was not always that way for me.

Growing Up with the Need to Please

People-pleasing started early for me. Before I was three years old, my little sister joined our family. Mom and Dad were my world, but for some reason, my mom was the center of it. I sought her approval then and have continued to do so for most of my life. When I went to the hospital to meet my little sister, the nurse on duty happened to be the same one who delivered me. As a gift for becoming a big sister, she gave me a new baby doll. Of all the names I could have chosen in the world, I chose the one I adored the most—Marilyn, my mother's name. I still remember the pride in her expression when she realized I'd named my new baby doll after her. I look back now and realize how odd it was, almost to the point of embarrassment. But my people-pleasing tendencies back then made it seem like a perfectly normal thing to do.

That was just the beginning of my need to please others. As I grew, my need to please extended beyond my family. Everyone I met was a new opportunity for friendship, and I was going to love him or her with everything in me. Oh, the innocence of young Dawn.

In those early, formative years, people-pleasing came in a variety of packages—and not always pretty ones. I adored my first grade teacher, Mrs. Diver. I had a lot of friends and excelled in school. First grade was a good year.

Right before second grade began, the school I attended discovered an asbestos problem. Our class was divided and transferred to other nearby elementary schools. I found myself in a new classroom with all new students and only three familiar faces. In a few summer months, my perfect world went from paradise to Armageddon. Okay, maybe that's an exaggeration, but it was bad. For the first time in my life, I was the butt of people's jokes. I experienced bullying on the playground, in the bathroom, and on the bus—anywhere away from the eyes of teachers. Students found ways to trip me up, call me names, and rattle my tender heart. Nearly every day, I went home crying after school.

I learned then that most people could not be trusted and that people I thought were my friends one day would turn their backs on me the next.

To protect my little heart, my little mind taught me to become what people wanted me to be. To act the way they wanted me to act, dress the way they wanted me to dress . . . all to win their approval. I became a chameleon: blending in, meeting expectations just to make others happy. In the process, I completely lost who I was. I soon believed the lie that it was more important to please people than to seek the pleasure of God.

Extrovert or Introvert

Most of my life, I was an extrovert. However, according to a post by Carol Bainbridge on Verywell.com, "Most people believe an extrovert is a person who is friendly and outgoing. While that may be true, it is not the true meaning of extroversion. An extrovert is a person who is energized by being around other people."[4]

According to the Myers-Briggs personality test, I was an ENFJ: Extrovert (E), Intuitive (N), Feeling (F), Judgment (J). From toddler to young adulthood, I sought out others to fill the internal cup of energy that kept me going. I busied my mind with obsessive-compulsive thoughts of what others were doing, what they were thinking, and whether they were talking about me. I spent my days overly involved in activities because if I was with people, there was more opportunity for me to please them, to feel their validation, and to know they were on my side when I was apart from them. I needed to be where the action was all the time. High school is a rough place to be when you have been made fun of a child, because teenagers can be brutal. Thankfully for me, high school meant new friendships. Those friendships kept me morally on track, until they didn't. As an approval addict who did not know God, it became particularly tricky to navigate life because friends and their opinions became my idols. Over time, my innocent hangouts with friends turned into weekend parties. I felt compelled to do the cool thing, even when it meant compromising my morals. That unhealthy behavior extended into college, where I reinvented myself, yet again. Far from parental boundaries, I partied almost every day of the week. I filled my social calendar with late nights and missed classes to the point of nearly flunking out of school. I ended my first semester with a 1.7 GPA.

I also joined organizations, and as the years went on, there were many. The mix of a low GPA and a good talking-to by my student government advisor was enough for me to get myself into gear academically. That, and the fact that the sorority I wanted to join required a 2.5 GPA for membership. I was forced to study, learn time management, and meet some higher academic standards. As a result, I received a scholarship after my second semester for "most improved GPA," going from a 1.7 to a 3.2.

After that, there was no stopping me. I was hell-bent on getting involved, getting voted into leadership positions, and receiving the affirmation of the people around me. I was going to prove everyone wrong. I was going to be everything I hadn't been in high school (but had always dreamed of being). Fellow students respected me as a leader and twice elected me as student body president. After a rigorous selection process, I was selected as a freshman orientation leader. In later years I was elected as Greek Council president. Great stuff, right? Except that I was still striving to near exhaustion to please the people around me and prove to myself that all those things once said of me were wrong.

I'm older now and maybe slightly wiser, and my perspective has changed. In fact, if I took the Myers-Briggs today, I would be an INFJ, a straight-up introvert. I am still a people person and very much enjoy the company of others. But these days, after spending time around people, especially in large groups, I need to retreat to gain back my energy. So, what changed?

Two things: a hefty dose of real life, and another dose of new life.

My fifth year of college was not spent alone. I had a committed boyfriend, whom I loved, but who also had some issues. We were in college, and that meant partying. For him, it meant times that he became highly inebriated; for me, it meant doing whatever he wanted me to do. When he was sober, life was not that bad. But when he was drunk, well, it became challenging.

I believed the lie that if I loved him enough, I could change him. I loved him so much, I accepted his proposal for marriage, moved in with him, and married him shortly after. After college, life did not change much and so, by the time I was twenty-five, I was divorced, depressed, and caught up in a vicious, destructive cycle. Finally, sheer desperation brought me to my knees.

At age twenty-six, I surrendered my people-pleasing heart and allowed God to transform me into a new creation. The old had gone, and the new had come. It took years of falling on my face and allowing Him to pick me up before I realized that filling my life with the expectations of others was never going to calm my racing heart. But when He taught me who I was, it stuck.

My energy used to flow from people because that energy came bottled up in their approval of me. I constantly obsessed over what they thought, always needed to have people around me, and never wanted to be alone. I was always worried I was missing something. Well, I was missing something all right, but it wasn't all those things I was filling my life with. It was Jesus.

I am pretty sure I am not the only who has been challenged with situations like I have described. Maybe, like me, you were bullied as a child. Maybe you faced challenges in middle or high school. Or maybe you are experiencing something like that right now. People-pleasing pressure has a way of intensifying as we start new chapters in our lives. Even as adults, we can feel like we must look or act a certain way. We feel pressure to marry the right person, find the perfect home, drive a certain type of car, and have 2.5 children. As grown women, we make it even worse for ourselves as we size up each other at work, social gatherings, and our children's sporting events. It's not any easier at church, either, as we compare our clothes, Bibles, or relationships with the woman sitting two rows away. We struggle with feeling accepted and find ourselves striving for the approval of others in our lives.

So often, we want nothing more than the approval of the people we care about—and instead we receive rejection, which can be devastating. Our deepest needs exist in the gap between seeking out the acceptance of someone and that same person's response to us. We have all believed the lie that happiness comes through pleasing others rather than finding the pleasure of our God.

Oh, and the challenges of social media only make matters worse for approval addicts. We get caught up in both the positive and the negative sides of people-pleasing, posting things to get likes or tearing down others with comments.

And the spread of technology exacerbates the challenge even further as new issues arise, like cyberbullying—as if being bullied in person was not enough. Now someone you may never have met can chime in on your picture, video, or post. Other people can post or tag you in unflattering pictures. Some people will even pronounce unkind judgments or try to start arguments with you through a friend's feed or page. For an approval addict, such actions are fraught with danger, inducing worry, fear, even depression and isolation.

A Brain Teaser

What happens to our brains when we seek to please others? And why is it so addictive? Our brains are wired to associate certain activities with pleasure. This wiring is referred to as a "reward circuit." It is activated when the brain notes something important or pleasurable that it wants to remember and reexperience.[5] The reward circuit releases dopamine, a brain chemical that makes us feel good, and that good feeling drives us to seek that reward over and over again. For example, when we eat, our body receives a reward and then desires that reward again when our stomach sends messages to the brain to feed our body. Overindulgence occurs when we begin to crave our next dopamine fix, overstimulating that reward circuit. In fact, a wide variety of addictions begin when we give in to the brain's cravings for that "fix" soon after the last one was processed.

This concept applies to the need for approval, particularly when it comes to social media. Every time we see something that pleases us, dopamine is released in our brain. Consider how frequently that can occur while scanning your news feed, reviewing your own posts, and seeing your likes or comments. The fact that our most popular Facebook posts move up to the top of our news feed only makes us strive even more to achieve approval from others.

Ever think to yourself in the middle of a bad day, "I need to check Facebook. Maybe that will make me feel better"? This happens when your brain needs a dopamine fix and, by golly, it's going to get it one way or another. We depend on all those likes and friends to make us feel better; we are addicted.

Social media plays with our mood, both positively and negatively. Did you know that there is now a condition called "Facebook depression"?[6] It shouldn't be all that shocking to us. Over time, drug addicts build up a resistance to their preferred drug. That means they must increase their usage to experience a high. The increasing need for more overwhelms the addict. They might want to quit more than anything, but their cravings make them physically ill. They feel relief only after they get their next dose.

In much the same way, approval addicts crave Facebook or other social stimuli. And just as the heroin addict starts to feel the dull pain of sobriety, we begin to feel the dull pains of comparison, jealousy, envy, and strife—all of which can lead to depression.

Two German universities joined forces to investigate social networking. Researchers discovered that one in three people they surveyed felt worse (lonely, frustrated, angry) after spending frequent time on Facebook, due to perceived inadequacies when comparing themselves to friends.[7]

Have you ever experienced that? Maybe you were casually checking out other people's lives on Facebook and, before you knew it, you were feeling like you needed a new hairstyle, a diet was in your near future, and you were going to start working out. Come to think of it, you decided your home really needed a makeover and your wardrobe needed updating ASAP—all in the span of about ten minutes! By the time you put down your phone or tablet, you were depressed because your life was not what it should be. Yet you pick up that device again, and your fingers just won't stop scrolling as you judge yourself based on those little snippets of other people's lives.

The more I think about it, it's shocking that only one in three users feel worse after using social media; it should *three* in three users. I suspect the other two are just in denial. We all struggle with comparing ourselves to others. We fall into the trap of idealizing other people and their things, and it affects our clothing choices, hairstyles, and even the way we design our homes. So, what are we to do?

There is a dichotomy at work here in which it feels like our lives are becoming more and more public, yet we are hiding behind screens. Our brains are triggered to enjoy our online experience; we want more and more of it because it gratifies the need to feel the approval of others, yet it can also make us feel deficient, defeated, or depressed. So how exactly are we supposed to respond to social media if we have this nature, this innate need to please others? How do we replace the lie that we need to please others and focus instead on seeking the smile of God?

If It Pleases the King

I remember exactly where I was sitting when God opened my eyes to my people-pleasing tendencies. It was the early fall of 2010, and I was studying the life of David. My husband, son, and I had just relocated from Ohio to my husband's hometown in Alabama. We moved there because we believed God wanted us to start a local church that focused on the needs of those who had left church or never experienced a church community. We also believed that God wanted to use us to break the cycle of poverty in our community. My husband was the church planter, worship leader, and visionary of the church. I was trying to support him in every way I could, but as a born-and-bred Yankee in the Deep South, I was also struggling to embrace life and find my place in this new setting.

Early in my life as a follower of Jesus, God gave me a heart for women. I am at ease when I am teaching about what I have learned in the Word of God, and I love helping other women gain clarity and freedom in their walk with Jesus. Although I knew those things, I was asking God to show me who He wanted me to become in this new place. How was I to minister to others when I knew nearly no one?

There at my table, God delivered the gut punch I needed to awaken me to my character flaw. Until then, I hadn't really understood the depth of my people-pleasing tendencies or the wounds that I was trying to disguise or heal.

David's story inspired this approval addict. Actually, it wasn't David alone who inspired me, but the vivid contrast between him and King Saul. Saul was the first king of Israel. He had been shown tremendous favor by God, yet the difference between him and the younger man, David, was like darkness and light.

The first time we read about David seeking God over man is in 1 Samuel. At the direction of his father, the shepherd boy David took food to his older brothers, who were on the front lines during the battles between the Israelites and the Philistines. The Philistines had with them a huge warrior who made the Israelites shake in their leather-strapped sandals. No one in the whole Israelite camp felt brave enough to go up against the giant, whose name was Goliath.

When David entered the camp and heard this news, he was indignant. He began telling everyone to quit being so afraid. He—a shepherd boy—was trying to pump up the army of God. When King Saul heard about this, he sent for David. First Samuel 17:32–37 tells us that David didn't back down, though he stood before a king.

"David said to Saul, 'Let no one lose heart on account of this Philistine; your servant will go and fight him.'

"Saul replied, 'You are not able to go out against the Philistine and fight him; you are only a young man, and he has been a warrior from his youth'" (vs. 32–33).

David then explained to Saul that many lions and bears had tried to attack his father's sheep, but he had defended the sheep and saved them from death. He continued, "This uncircumcised Philistine will be like one of them, because he has defied the armies of the living God. The LORD who rescued me from the paw of the lion and the paw of the bear will rescue me from the hand of this Philistine" (vv. 36–37).

I picture the king shrugging as he answered. "Go, and the LORD be with you" (v. 37b).

David was bold and secure in who he was because he knew what his God could do. He didn't question or tremble with worry or fear. He did not try to please others—not even the king! He knew what was at stake. Lives were on the line, and his defense was God. Only God.

If you have spent much time reading the Bible or listening to Bible stories, you know that David went on to defeat Goliath. He took him out with a sling and a single stone. One shot was all he needed. David was the hero that day as he took out Goliath and helped the Israelite army defeat the Philistines. David's story reminds us that when we focus on God and what He can do, we need no longer seek to please man.

Saul, however, was a different man altogether. As a young man he was tall, dark, and handsome—and incredibly insecure. He questioned who he was and later even questioned his anointing as king. Before long, his choices and his actions followed his thinking.

Instead of trusting God and knowing that God was able to accomplish things Saul could not, he was ruled by fear. Saul saw himself as incapable of being God's anointed king. He worried about what other people thought rather than what God wanted. This, unfortunately, cost him his position as king. First Samuel 15 relates that God dispatched the prophet Samuel to reject Saul as king because he had once again sought to please other humans rather than patiently seeking the Lord. When Samuel confronted him, King Saul answered: "I have sinned. I violated the LORD's command and your instructions. I was *afraid* of the men and so I gave in to them" (1 Samuel 15:24, emphasis added).

Saul's fear of men kept him from obeying God and lost him the very position he was anointed to fulfill, while David, though he certainly had his fair share of trials, became known as "a man after [God's] own heart" (1 Samuel 13:14). For people-pleasers, there is freedom in that statement; each of us can become a man or woman "after God's own heart"—we have no need to please everyone around us.

At that point in my study, I realized my people-pleasing needed to stop. If God was ever going to use me, I would have to be more like David and seek only the pleasure of God. I needed to stop letting fear make me focus on how others felt about me. My job was to obey God, not others, and to seek the pleasure of God instead of caring about the opinions of mere men and women. But it took time for me to make that shift. It took effort to get over my fears.

What about you? Do you feel more like Saul, who allowed his fear of what man thought to rule him and keep him from obeying God, or David, who knew he was a son of God and acted out of that identity with courage and determination? A Saul mentality may feel easier or natural to you than a David mentality, but it is also limiting and even destructive. So, how do we get from a Saul mentality to a David mentality?

Reading this book is a good first step in realizing how deep your need to please people can go. What if, like Saul, you have also been anointed to a position? You don't want to realize too late that you chose pleasing others instead of obeying the God who created you and loves you, right?

To make this needed change, you must experience a paradigm shift in your thinking. Every day and in every situation, you must seriously consider whether you are seeking to please man or God. Get into the habit of asking yourself—even out loud—"Am I seeking to obey man in this, or God? Am I seeking my own glory, or am I seeking to bring glory to God?"

Paul questioned himself in Galatians 1:10: "Am I now trying to win the approval of human beings, or of God? Or am I trying to please people? If I were still trying to please people, I would not be a servant of Christ."

If you have accepted Jesus Christ as your Lord and Savior, you have taken on a new identity as a servant of Christ, a child of the Most High God, and an heir to His throne. As such, you have not been given a "spirit of fear; but of power, and of love, and of a sound mind" (2 Timothy 1:7 KJV).

When we are secure in the knowledge that we are God's children, we will realize that no one's approval matters more than His. Just as I used to spend energy seeking the approval of my parents as a child, I now take that energy to seek the approval of my heavenly Father, knowing that His approval already rests on me. It's all I truly need.

That's the first step in becoming a God-pleaser: Decide that His pleasure is more important to you than anything else and live your life considering His perspective on all matters. I have heard it said many times that the Bible is our instruction guide for life. That may be true, but I prefer to see the Bible as the revelation of God's heart and His desire for us. Sure, it can come in the form of instructions, but who likes to read instructions?

When you consider how the Bible uncovers the truth of who our God is and who we are in Him, reading and studying it becomes an adventure. As you uncover these truths, you will begin to see how His nature can be reflected in your own life. And that reflection will not resemble what Facebook or other social media tell you.

Society pushes you to strive for the next best thing; God tells you to be content no matter what the circumstance (Philippians 4:11). Society tells you to seek after the treasures of this world; God tells you to pursue treasures in heaven (Mark 10:21). Social media tells you to obsess about what others think; God tells you not to worry about anything but simply bring your requests to Him and let Him take care of you (Philippians 4:6).

We can walk in this "new and living way" (Hebrews 10:20), knowing we are not alone. Together we can overcome the addiction to approval, the need to please others. It will be a process, one that will require us to be patient with ourselves. But there is more power in *together* than there ever is *alone*. Seek out an accountability partner. Set a goal for this year to start studying Scripture and learning the truth of who you are. Make it your mission to destroy every lie, every stronghold, and every barrier the enemy has put up to encourage you to please man. Together, we can become women after God's own heart. Together we can experience freedom. Together we can stop striving to please people and instead rest in the pleasure of God.

Lord Jesus, I want to rely on Your Word, so I can better know who I am. I want to get better at identifying the lies the enemy has told me. I want to stop conforming to who this world thinks

I should be. In doing so, I ask You to change my heart in the same way You changed David's, so I will be known as a woman after Your own heart. Help me not to seek the approval or pleasure of those around me, but to seek to please You with my whole being. I want to stop striving to be like others; I want to model myself after You. You have not given me a spirit of fear, but one of power, love, and a sound mind. Guide me as I go about my days, so that when I need affirmation, I seek it from You and You alone. In Your holy and precious name I pray, amen.

Me, Insecure?

· · · · · · · · · · ·

I have insecurities, of course, but I don't hang out
with anyone who points them out to me.

ADELE

L aura exuded self-confidence. She was beautiful, kind, and smart. Everyone liked her. Boys would nearly fall at her feet, yet she acted as if she barely knew they existed. I don't think she dated anyone until high school. By that point she was a cheerleader and top-seeded tennis player, in honors classes, on the homecoming court, and later elected prom queen. I am pretty sure Laura got into her first-choice college with no problems at all. I envied her. She seemed to have nothing to be insecure about, which was a distant dream for me.

I was Laura's opposite, as insecure as they come. I questioned myself constantly and often wondered whether my friends were truly my friends. I earned Cs in school (at best, Bs), and started high school in the marching band. The cool girls were cheerleaders or played hockey and lacrosse; I played the flute and dreamed of being talented enough to make an athletic team. Oh sure, I caught the attention of a few boys, but my insecurities made me question their motives. I sought their attention but never thought I was worthy of it.

My insecurities got me in trouble more than once as a teenager. My self-confidence and sense of worth were wrapped up in the things I did or did not have. I placed significance on positions and titles, social statuses, and academic achievement. Because I didn't meet my own expectations in those areas, I saw myself as less than those I perceived as successful. I constantly strove for more, always needed more attention, more friends, more validation from the people around me. But because I lacked confidence and contentment in who I was, nothing I did, no one I hung out with, and no position I ever held was enough. I look back now and think I must have exhausted everyone around me. My constant need for approval had turned into a full-blown addiction.

This continued into college, where my addiction only got worse. By then, I had learned to cover up my insecurities through social activities and social status. My life was significantly different in college as compared to high school, my continued lack of confidence deepened the need to keep striving for more. I acted confident, but it was a façade, and as I grew better at faking it, my "confidence" morphed into bossy and controlling behavior. I manipulated situations to make them work for my benefit, as if I had everything together. All the while, insecurities ate me up inside.

I had achieved a lot while I was in college and had become a respected student leader, but it wasn't until my fourth year that I finally declared a major. At first, I thought I'd study criminal justice and become a lawyer like my cousin. Then I thought maybe I'd do secondary education English, like a boy I was dating, or perhaps business like one of my sorority sisters. After taking courses in each of those majors, however, I knew I needed to pick something else. I'd already decided on a career in counseling college students and didn't need a specific major for that goal, so I chose to major in what I enjoyed most: writing.

That decision changed everything. For the first time, I couldn't fake it. I'd always loved journaling and now had also written what I thought were decent college papers. People told me I had a way with words, so I figured a professional writing major made sense . . . until I started taking classes. I was not as good as I thought I was. Not by a long shot. I went from being a B student to struggling to maintain Cs. I experienced the editing process for the first time . . . and it was an excruciating process. Had I not needed to just graduate with a degree, I would have changed my major. But I decided to commit to it.

Those two years (yes, I did five years of college) were the hardest of my college career. I couldn't fake confidence anymore; I had none. Almost every paper I submitted was torn to pieces. I would make improvements only to find myself questioning nearly everything I had written. To graduate, I had to fulfill an internship and successfully complete my senior thesis class, which included a senior portfolio and a comprehensive exam. My senior thesis class was taught by one of the hardest English professors in the department, and I had selected the second hardest professor, the department chair, for my internship. There is nothing like two experts to keep you insecure and on your toes.

The internship was intense. I worked for the student activities office, and the director was a grammar guru. She made me edit my work a minimum of fifteen times each project before the final product was complete. Her usual comment on my pieces was, "Details, details, details." Details would be the difference between achieving an A or an F.

I worked hard to put together my portfolio and prepare for the comprehensive exam. My professor told me from the start I would be lucky to pass this class since I had declared the major so late and most of my peers had been professional writing majors since they were freshmen. I was at a severe disadvantage and had to work hard to prove I could become a professional writer. I worked relentlessly to create a portfolio that would include my best writing from freshman to senior year. We were specifically told not to change anything from prior years, as the portfolio review committee, made up of other professors, would want to see how we had progressed over time.

Did I mention I was at a severe disadvantage? Since I had not been a professional writing major from the beginning, I struggled to locate papers I had written in the early years. Further, I was the only person who had edited my work, and I had already learned that was not good enough. On the other hand, my peers had learned and grown through the professors' feedback over four years.

I submitted my best work, and hoped the review committee and my professor would see that it did have value. But when I went for my final portfolio appointment, my fears became reality. His words are as real today as they were when he spoke them to me over twenty years ago: "This portfolio only proves what we already knew. You do not have what it takes to become a professional writer. You will never be a published author. You might as well find another profession altogether, because no one in his right mind would pay you for your work."

I wish I could tell you that quote is a cruel exaggeration. But my professor felt it was his job to make it clear who could write professionally and who could not. He was clear: I could not.

As you might imagine, I was crushed. All I had left was the fact that I was one of the few in the senior thesis class who had passed the comprehensive exams and the hope that my internship portfolio had gone better than my senior portfolio. My internship supervisor in student activities had given me an A for my performance, so it was up to my assigned internship professor to decide whether I needed to seek another career.

My internship portfolio sat with several others in a box outside her office. I remember carefully removing mine and sitting on the floor next to the box, debating whether I should open it. I thought about taking it home and allowing someone else to see the grade before me. But I decided if my fate was a shattered dream, I should take it alone in this empty hallway. I slowly opened the binder. An A– greeted me from the top of the page! I refrained from shouting but did a happy dance from my seated position . . . and then I saw the sticky note attached to the page. The note included my name and my grade and the phrase, "Who would have ever thought it could be possible."

I had earned an A–, but there was that statement: "Who would have ever thought it could be possible." The whole world was against me. I would have to decide where I was going to go from here. There was nothing and no one left to encourage me. I had no hope of ever becoming a professional writer. Talk about insecurities! I was about to graduate with a degree, but according to my professors, it would never amount to anything at all. I was devastated.

I decided I would avoid a writing career. I tried to get a job in counseling and advising students, but the interview process proved disastrous. I had a résumé filled with student leader responsibilities and experiences, but I felt like an imposter. I had a BA in professional writing, but it had nothing to do with the jobs for which I interviewed. I eventually accepted a job as a floor manager at a department store.

All the work I had done to prove people wrong, all the time I'd spent learning to be a leader, the countless hours of trying to improve my writing craft and find my voice—they all came crashing down around me. I decided that I was exactly what every negative remark about me had said I was. I would never amount to anything. Period. I believed that my worth was defined by who I thought I was. I decided I was less than my peers and gave up completely.

We do this to ourselves all the time, don't we? We allow outside circumstances or individuals to define who we are and what we are destined to become. We hear the thoughts and opinions of others and allow those words to define us. I've realized over the years how this has become the enemy's ammunition in my life. Let me walk you through what this looks like for me. Maybe you can relate.

Someone makes a remark about a deficiency in my life, and it rings true, at least as far as who I believe I am. Until that moment, I hadn't realized anyone but me knew about that flaw. I feel exposed, as if now *everyone* is aware of the fact that I am less. For example, someone might observe, "You are not very good at delegating. I have never seen anyone as controlling as you are."

Whether the person is right or wrong does not matter. I've internalized their statement as truth, and fear and anxiety rise inside of me because I've been exposed. I am not perfect, not even close. I feel shame and guilt. I feel helpless to change. I am embarrassed that I am not who that person expected me to be, and I now want to hide from the world. The mask is off and the world can see the real me.

Oh, but that's not the end of it. I begin harboring negative thoughts about the other person. Rather than going back to the person and asking for clarification or considering that maybe the comment came from his or her own stresses or insecurities, I begin tearing down that person in my head. I weigh my critic's weaknesses against my own—but instead of making myself feel better, I end up distancing myself from that person and from God, as I sin against both.

I begin to see everyone around me in a negative light. I become bitter and angry, pointing out other people's flaws and shortcomings. I am the judge of all things, and I have little mercy. I deflect my emotions about the situation onto other people who are completely innocent because I am now assuming they feel the same way about me as the other person. They've all been conspiring to show me who I really am.

My prayer life suffers. I lose interest in spending time with God or doing God-centered things because, well, He's probably going to reveal more of my shortcomings. I become increasingly prideful; I dig in my heels and rationalize my behavior. The shame and guilt build, isolating me further from God and other people.

And then what do I do? I begin to beat myself up. I feel less than other people, I realize how much I don't like myself, and I come to the conclusion that my critic was probably correct. In fact, in my imagination, I make myself appear even worse. I consider quitting whatever it is I am leading. My insecurities fester, even as my awareness of my own unworthiness makes me feel still more unworthy.

I typically land in one of two camps at this point: Either I decide to end this pity party and seek God for wisdom and guidance, or I begin feeling utterly depressed. If I have any presence of mind at this point, I will remember that I can choose repentance and allow it to break me out of this horrible cycle. I know I could experience emotions like joy, peace, and hope—if only I decide to agree with God's Word and submit to what the Holy Spirit tells me to do.

Unfortunately, it is a cycle, and the cycle can begin again with another person's remarks or some other trigger. The cycle looks something like this:

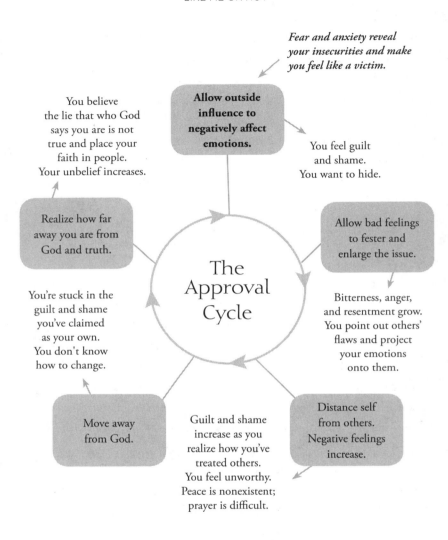

Fear and anxiety reveal your insecurities and make you feel like a victim.

Allow outside influence to negatively affect emotions.

You feel guilt and shame. You want to hide.

You believe the lie that who God says you are is not true and place your faith in people. Your unbelief increases.

Realize how far away you are from God and truth.

The Approval Cycle

Allow bad feelings to fester and enlarge the issue.

You're stuck in the guilt and shame you've claimed as your own. You don't know how to change.

Bitterness, anger, and resentment grow. You point out others' flaws and project your emotions onto them.

Move away from God.

Guilt and shame increase as you realize how you've treated others. You feel unworthy. Peace is nonexistent; prayer is difficult.

Distance self from others. Negative feelings increase.

Can you relate? Do you do this to yourself? Do you allow the enemy to determine your moods, actions, emotional stability, the health of your relationships, and even your future, all because you get caught up in the lies that say you are not worthy, that you are less than others, that you can't possibly have any purpose or place here on Planet Earth?

If so, you are not alone. But don't despair—God tells you differently. His Word teaches that you have worth, purpose, and confidence in Him.

Defining Insecurity

Joseph Nowinski, author of *The Tender Heart: Conquering Your Insecurity*, writes:

> Insecurity refers to a profound sense of self-doubt—a deep feeling of uncertainty about our basic worth and our place in the world. Insecurity is associated with chronic self-consciousness, along with chronic lack of confidence in ourselves and anxiety about our relationships. The insecure man or woman lives in constant fear of rejection and a deep uncertainty about whether his or her own feelings and desires are legitimate.[8]

When we question everything about ourselves, sizing ourselves up and comparing ourselves with others, we are exhibiting insecure behaviors. We are afraid of what others think, and we second-guess (or even third-guess) our response in nearly every situation. As a result, sometimes we feel we are less than someone else, and sometimes we puff ourselves up as we tear down another person.

That is the backhandedness of insecurity—it can make us feel *less than* or drive us to try to look *more than*. Either way, we are hiding our true selves, the people God created us to be.

In a social-media context, the insecure woman might critically read through her posts and analyze others. She decides what is good and what is bad, then she takes what she likes and mimics it in her own posts in the hope that others will like or share her post—even if the post doesn't reflect her ideas or opinions much at all. Sometimes she will poll people on a certain situation, hoping her friends will side with her. She may seek affirmation about her body, position, purchases, personality, and so on. Social media is a drug for the insecure person; it soothes and salves temporarily, even while it creates more dependence. It never fully satisfies, no matter what it promises.

So how can we who are caught in this addiction ever feel or act differently? How do we break the cycle of harboring ill thoughts, hiding behind feelings of shame and guilt, becoming bitter and angry, and ultimately distancing ourselves from God and others? Is there a way to avoid the emotions and actions that separate us from prayer and time in the Word? Is there a way out of the pit of despair we've dug for ourselves? Will the cycle ever stop?

Yes, you can learn to identify and anticipate the patterns. You can break the cycle. However, you need to know this up front: The battle will never stop. It is a tactic of your enemy to defame your character, to obscure your likeness to your heavenly Father. You must understand the attack is not against you alone—it is also against God. But you can learn how to respond to the attacks at every stage. If you will stick with it and persevere and gather and sharpen the weapons you need to defeat the enemy's attacks, you will experience victory in this area. So let's not delay any longer. Let's see what God says about who you are and how your worth and confidence is established and complete in Him.

Defining Confidence

Let's take a journey back in time to the first man and first woman, Adam and Eve. There in the garden, we can see where our insecurities, our fear of rejection, and the attack on our worth began. Genesis 1:27 tells us that God created man and woman *in His own image*. This is extremely important in our understanding of where our worth and confidence come from. Knowing it should inform our response.

We were created in God's image—we are mirror images of our

God! Said another way, we are image bearers. We bear the likeness of God in a way no other part of Creation does—not the angels, not the demons, not animals, nor the landscape. Nothing else in all of creation is like us in that respect. To be human is to be like God: your spirit, character, sense of humor, emotions, and mind somehow all resemble the God who created you.

No wonder Satan attacked Eve's worth and confidence. If you look at Genesis 3 (the account of the fall of those first humans into sin), you will see how the serpent successfully exposed Eve's insecurities and thus brought about the chain of events that separated humans from God. Genesis 3:1 ESV says:

> Now the serpent was more crafty than any other beast of the field that the LORD God had made. He said to the woman, "Did God actually say, 'You shall not eat of any tree in the garden'?"

The serpent's words may be the most loaded question in history: *"Did God actually say . . .?"* The question attacked Eve's confidence in God, and it made her doubt herself, her husband, her memory, and her ability to make a decision. It questions her worth and purpose as a caretaker of the garden; it makes her wonder if she is doing a good job or if perhaps she is not doing all that she should be doing. It attacks her confidence in Adam, because he must have been the one who relayed the commandment to her. In Genesis 2:15–17 ESV we read:

> The LORD God took the man and put him in the garden of Eden to work it and keep it. *And the LORD God commanded the man,* saying, "You may surely eat of every tree of the garden, but of the tree of the knowledge of good and evil you

shall not eat, for in the day that you eat of it you shall surely die." [Emphasis added.]

The command was given before Eve was created! The serpent struck at a point that probably was most likely to insert doubt and incite insecurity.

All these are tactics of the enemy. In John 10:10 ESV, Jesus said that our enemy "comes only to steal and kill and destroy." This is just one example of how he accomplishes that mission.

The serpent in the garden called into question the perfection of God's creation. He began by questioning Adam and Eve's capabilities as caretakers. Today he does the same thing to us. Do we know who—and whose—we are? Do we know what we have been given to steward, or are we confused about our purpose? Do we understand the power within us, or do we see ourselves as powerless?

The question, "Did God really say . . .?" undermines our sense of security in God. It's hard to imagine Adam and Eve having any insecurities—after all, they wandered around the garden naked! (It makes me blush just thinking about it.) But their response to the serpent's questions show how much they were like us. Eve reasoned with the serpent and allowed uncertainty to creep into her thoughts. (And oh, yeah, the fruit looked good too.)

Imagine the thoughts going through Eve's mind: "Do I believe what God told Adam, or do I believe this serpent? What will happen if I don't agree with this serpent? How will the serpent respond to me? Will the serpent believe I know what I am talking about? Do I even *know* what I'm talking about?" Eve was just as human as we are—and she was feeling a little insecure, a little off-kilter. She wanted to please the creature in front of her just as we would.

I could almost transcribe this from the soundtrack that often runs in my mind. Our insecurities make us vulnerable to peer pressure. Peer pressure can lead to purchasing more than we should on a shopping trip because our friends insisted we just *had to have* that dress, though we knew it was out of our budget. Peer pressure cuts our hair the way someone else likes it; it convinces us to wear clothes we otherwise would have rejected. *"Did he really say . . .?"*

The enemy is cunning; he delights in provoking us to forget who we are and where our self-worth comes from. "Do you really know who you are? Are you secure and confident in that knowledge, or can I make you question it?"

Eve did.

You recall what happened next. She saw the fruit—it was "good for food and pleasing to the eye, and also desirable for gaining wisdom"—and she ate it. (Genesis 3:6). Then she gave it to her husband and he ate it. Then they hid. God pursued them and found them (as if He didn't know where they were). Even in such times, God makes Himself known as our pursuer.

When God called them to account for their actions, Adam and Eve did much as we would do—they played the blame game: "He made me do it; she made me do it; the snake made us do it." Their sin separated them from God, and they chose blame instead of repentance. This confirmed their insecurities and revealed that they didn't know their identity in God at all and, therefore, could not have any confidence in Him.

And that's the cycle: The enemy attacks our worth, significance, and purpose. That in turn reveals our insecurities. We feel shame and guilt and hide ourselves from others and God. We blame instead of repent, we distance ourselves further from God, feeling more shame and more guilt until we suffer the consequences of isolation, depression, or worse. It isn't until we realize the need to change our behaviors and reconcile with Him and others through repentance that we can break the cycle.

Taking Forward Steps

It's easy to see that Eve shared our struggle, that she felt the same need for approval we do. I don't want us to leave this story before we realize her struggle began because Eve forgot or ignored who she was and whose she was. This is the same thing that makes us feel insecure today. When we don't know who we are, we become easy prey for our enemy.

So that is step one. We must know that we are under attack from a spiritual enemy, not one made of flesh and blood; we wrestle "against evil rulers and authorities of the unseen world, against mighty powers in this dark world, and against evil spirits in the heavenly places" (Ephesians 6:12 NLT). The enemy uses people to attack us where it hurts the most, but he is an evil spirit and he has one goal, to oppose God. If he can defame the created, he can defame the Creator, and he will do that using the people around us.

Further, we, with our weaknesses, insecurities, and wounds, can be used by the enemy to lie to others, which can undermine or destroy their relationships with God, isolating them and ultimately confirming their insecurities and promoting the lie that they cannot rely on God. So, the first step is to *recognize the attack and the attacker.* In doing so, we'll no longer see the person as our enemy; we'll recognize instead the spiritual powers behind their actions. And we'll know better how to fight because we'll know who we are fighting.

The next step is to *remind ourselves of who we are and whose we are.* When the serpent tempted Eve, she could have responded differently. She might have said, "Excuse me, I don't know who you are or why you're talking to me, but I know who I am. I am a unique creation of God. I'm His child, and my job is not to debate the details of what He said but simply to partner with my husband in caring for the garden. So right now, using the good brain God gave me, I think this garden needs some snake repellant." She didn't have to question her role, her purpose, or her identity as a daughter of God. She could have stuck to what she knew, first and foremost—that she was created in the image of God. Genesis 1:27 makes three distinct statements about this: "So God created mankind in his own image, in the image of God he created them; male and female he created them." The text leaves no doubt that we were made by the hand of God in His image.

Is God insecure in who He is? Absolutely not. In Exodus 3:14, He simply but boldly states, "I AM WHO I AM." God never questions His identity; He knows who He is. As image bearers, we can do the same, standing firm in who we are as His creation. At the end of this chapter is a list of Scriptures that clearly state who we are in Christ. Memorize them, so that when an attack on your identity comes, you can remind yourself by saying, "I know who I am and whose I am. I have nothing to be insecure about, because *He* has redeemed me."

The third step is to *realize that guilt and shame do not come from God.* Though the people of ancient Israel had broken God's heart with their sins and earned for themselves a long exile, God promised them, through the prophet Isaiah: "Instead of your shame you will receive a double portion, and instead of disgrace you will rejoice in your inheritance. And so you will inherit a double portion in your land, and everlasting joy will be yours" (Isaiah 61:7). You needn't wallow in shame and condemnation; those things do not come from God. You can live in the reality of the inheritance that comes through faith in God—qualities like joy, peace, healing, and redemption.

But what if you forget or ignore these steps and get caught up again in the same old cycle? Well, then, go to the next step: *forgiveness.* Realize that the person who hurt you or ignited your insecurities did so out of their own wounds. Intentional or not, it was because of their own wounds that they wounded you. You know what it's like to be caught in the cycle of approval addiction, wanting to lash out at others because you have been hurt; they may be in the same place. Their actions may have had nothing to do with you at all. Of course, there may be some degree of truth in what the person said or did. You are not perfect, but you can acknowledge this without falling prey to guilt and shame. In fact, you could even see their words or actions as a prompt for you to forgive another person (or yourself).

Either way, choosing this route rather than denial and hiding and blaming defeats the enemy and preserves your relationship with God. If you have hurt others in this process, go back and ask for forgiveness. As hard as that is sometimes, remember that pride doesn't like forgiveness; in the long run, you will experience healing and freedom as you practice forgiveness. As Scripture says, "Make allowance for each other's faults, and forgive anyone who offends you. Remember, the Lord forgave you, so you must forgive others" (Colossians 3:13 NLT).

Practicing forgiveness and grace toward others helps to break the cycle of addiction to approval.

Redefining Confidence

Once you learn you don't have to give in to insecurity, you can grow in the realization that security and confidence come from God. I know this to be true, through my own healing in this area. Just as I was about to write this book, the enemy attacked me at a very vulnerable spot. In the process, I realized how much God had taught me over the last few years. I was able to clearly identify the cycle I had been in. I avoided the knee-jerk reaction I was used to and moved into counterattack mode as soon as the attack began.

In years past, an attack like that would have sent me into a downward spiral. I would have spoken negatively of my attacker, coaxed others to take my side, and sought to justify my response so I could look better than her. I would have become bitter and angry, then the shame and regret for my actions would have placed distance between me and God. I would have placed all the blame on the woman who'd attacked me and not recognized the enemy's role in the situation at all. A slew of repercussions would have followed—I'd have withdrawn from her and all associations with her, which might also have meant I'd have to let go of my responsibilities in that area. I would have made matters worse by attacking her in public arenas, just as she had done to me on social media and elsewhere.

But I didn't, because God, in His grace and mercy, had taught me to do otherwise. I know who I am and whose I am, so I knew she attacked me out of her own wounds. Thus, I gave no weight to her remarks. She was hurt, and she wanted to hurt me. That was all.

What if we were all healed from our insecurities, and secure and confident in God's purpose for our lives? What if we no longer lashed out at others, wounding them and hurting ourselves in the process? What if we walked in the power and authority God has given to us through the Holy Spirit? What if we took the words the enemy said to Eve—"Did God really say . . . ?—and answered, "Yes, God really did say I am a child of God,[9] an heir to His throne.[10] I am a part of a royal priesthood,[11] set apart by Him to do good works that He designed for me to do because I am called according to His purpose.[12]" We could praise Him then for turning our mourning into celebration;[13] we could trade our insecurities for confidence in Him.

Go. Get into the Word of God and pull out the Scriptures that tell you more of who you are in Him. Start memorizing them. To help you get started, I have placed some Scriptures at the end of this chapter and in the Appendix in the back of this book. Get them into your mind and heart so that you'll have the weapons you need to stand firm and triumph. Rise up. You have been created in His image. He has designed you to walk in His power and authority for such a time as this.

Jesus, oh, how we love You. Your Word is perfect for every situation and against every attack from our enemy. Your life shows us what confidence in God looks like. You never questioned who You were; You always knew. Even when the enemy tried to tempt You in the desert, You knew Your place in the Trinity. You teach us that, as image bearers, we are full of the power and authority that the Holy Spirit provides. We can use that power to defeat our enemy. We can know who we are, having full confidence in our identity in You. Thank You, Jesus; we trust in Your holy and precious name. Amen.

Memorization Scriptures

But you are a chosen people, a royal priesthood, a holy nation, God's special possession, that you may declare the praises of him who called you out of darkness into his wonderful light.
1 Peter 2:9

For we are God's masterpiece.
He has created us anew in Christ Jesus,
so we can do the good things he planned for us long ago.
Ephesians 2:10 NLT

For in Christ Jesus you are all
sons (daughters) of God, through faith.
Galatians 3:26 ESV

No longer do I call you servants, for the servant does not know what his master is doing; but I have called you friends, for all that I have heard from my Father I have made known to you.
John 15:15 ESV

CHAPTER 4

My Way or the Highway

· · · · · · · · · · ·

As long as everything is exactly the way I want it,
I am totally flexible.

ROTTEN ECARDS

I have a problem: I need to be in control. All the time. It's been an
ongoing problem for months, years, even. Okay, my whole life.
It's why I always needed to play the role of teacher, mother, or leader.
I've often explained it away due to my type A personality or that I am
just a natural leader. It's who I am, right? I need to accept myself as
such. But what happens when who I am is not consistent with who
God's Word says I am? Then what? Do I stick with it just because, or
do I choose to change and become a better version of myself?

I have a theory; see if you agree. I think God uses our circumstances to remind us that we are not in control. In fact, I believe that
the more uncertain we are of those circumstances, the more God can

teach us how to "let go and let Him" so He can do what needs to be done. When we relinquish our desire to control to Him, we get to experience our place in His best and perfect plan.

Why do I believe this? I learned the hard way, by God not doing what I wanted Him to do when I wanted Him to do it. Been there? Here's how it can happen. A situation presents itself. I almost immediately decide the outcome I want but also decide I need to pray and wait on God's response. Then I try to manipulate God into the answer I want by arranging people or situations so I get what I want, when I want, and how I want.

Approval addicts struggle in this area because in our addiction, we have already planned out what we believe must take place for us to gain the approval we constantly seek. We will do whatever it takes to get our next approval fix, even if that means taking God or other people out of the equation.

Control issues and approval addictions go together seamlessly. As with any kind of addiction, you can never get enough. And because you never have enough approval, you will try to get it however you can—which usually means controlling God and others.

I Didn't Mean to Do That

Let's say you are in a meeting, and you've offered a suggestion that can improve the execution of a project. You feel hesitancy toward your idea from the people around you. You try to make eye contact to gain their approval, hoping to direct the outcome in your favor. (At times, that means overstating your opinion about an idea or driving the point home repeatedly until it wears people down.) Oh, but this is just a low level of approval. The true approval addict knows there is more approval to be had, if she can keep up the momentum.

Sensing the tone of the group, the approval addict begins to understand that she's going to need a higher level of approval from the group. Like a shark in bloody waters, the approval addict seeks her next opportunity to sink her teeth into an unsuspecting victim. Before Tommy knows it, he's been strong-armed into agreeing with her in nearly every area—which makes the kill even sweeter. If she can sway the entire group, she has accomplished her goal. When she does, it whets her appetite for still more. She feels confident, affirmed, and able to conquer the world. At the same time, she is oblivious to the casualties. She leaves the room victorious, but people have been used (and probably feel abused) . . . and the results may not even be in the best interests of her employer.

But that doesn't matter—our approval addict got her fix, and everything's good in her world. Control is a nasty game, often played "to the pain," to borrow a phrase from *The Princess Bride*.

I have been that person many more times than I would like to admit. I have been the controlling leader who thought she had to have all the best ideas, all the answers, and all the right words so everyone would think she was the best thing since *Fixer Upper* came to HGTV.

I was largely unaware of this control game until someone called me on it one day. Approval addicts tend to be oblivious to their need to control situations. Until they admit they have a problem, they don't see the real issues. They can't see why more people don't see life the way they do. But being called out was one of those "stop and look at yourself in the mirror" moments for me. I had to understand the person I had become and decide whether it was who I wanted to be.

Called on the Carpet

After graduate school, I took a job at Miami University in Oxford, Ohio. I became one of the assistant directors of Greek Life, designated as the Interfraternity Council Advisor to thirty-one fraternities. I was a twenty-six-year-old single woman who was, as my husband would say, "as lost as a billy goat." I had no clue at that point how badly I needed God. Four years later and still at that job, I was thirty years old, in love with Jesus, and had found my sweetheart for life and gotten married. My priorities had shifted. I was still young in my faith and trying to understand who I was in Christ. I wanted a job that wasn't so intense and time consuming.

I left the Greek Life position for one as an assistant director in the Office of Admission. Five of us served as assistant directors, with more than twenty staff members total. I was responsible for all major event planning, advising the college's student ambassadors, and recruiting students from a territory centered in Cleveland, Ohio. This position seemed like a dream come true for me. I'd discovered my love and talent for event planning after planning my own wedding, and I was excited to bring this talent into my work life.

Pretty quickly, however, I discovered that the environment and expectations of the admission office would require some adjustment on my part. Compared to the Greek Life office, the Office of Admission moved at a glacial pace. Major parts of my job required approvals from other people, and those approvals took time—lots and lots of time. My internal drive for perfection and the approval that perfection brings kept me plowing ahead. I wanted every detail in place and every aspect of every event to be perfect.

Planning the first time around was a bit rough. Planning my wedding was very different from planning an open house for a couple thousand people, including every major department at the university, several high-level leadership positions, the entire admission office, and every accepted college student and his or her parents. Everyone had an opinion on how the event should go, and they were quick to share those opinions with the new girl on the job. Department chairs didn't like my suggested changes, and they all had their own agendas when they pulled me aside to tell me so. Younger staff members were excited for the changes, while older staff thought we should leave well enough alone. I didn't understand why a few changes to achieve a smoother, high-class event would have become such a huge, controversial deal.

After much deliberation, it was suggested that, since I had not executed this event before, I should just leave it alone this time and not make major changes. The changes to this event were not worth the battle it was creating, they said. Being the approval addict I was, this felt like defeat. But I did as I was told.

With my time freed up a little, I had the summer to focus my energies on fall events. I was determined to make this my opportunity to shine. Red Carpet Day was coming up, an event where the university honored academically successful high school students. While we recognized their accomplishments, we would point out our own successes and try to woo them to our school. Miami University is known as a "public Ivy," a public school capable of producing an Ivy League educational experience. Our median GPA at the time was 3.3. We took "the next best" of the best—those students who didn't get into an Ivy League school. Red Carpet Day primed the pump for early admissions, and we did our best to lay down the proverbial red carpet for our guests.

I decided that, with fewer players involved, I could take this event to the next level and show my bosses and all those other folks just what I was capable of. I got the thumbs-up from my director and associate director. Most of our leadership team loved the enhancements I proposed. To accomplish my goals, however, I had to have the administrative staff on board. I needed their help.

I remember praying about how to communicate my ideas in a way that would gain their approval, so I could make the day special (and make myself look good). Unfortunately, I quickly found myself in the same battle again—the new girl proposing changes to a group of people who weren't interested in changing. Arguments against me ranged from the amount of time involved in planning when work schedules were already too busy to why we even needed to change a method that had worked in the past. This time, I refused to accept "no" for an answer.

With my director's support in my back pocket, so to speak, I began to get a little bossy about my needs. Okay, okay, I was downright impatient. I was tired of having the same conversation over and over. It was time for everyone involved to get on the new and improved Red Carpet Day train, because it was leaving the station.

The event invitation had to be reviewed and printed before I could get it in the mail. We were adding a thin red ribbon, looped into a straight line, into each invitation to add a punch. The ribbon made it almost look like the red carpet was in their hands. We had to insert the ribbon by hand, and that would take time. It was important that we stick to a tight timeline to accomplish the task on schedule. I emailed the invitation to the director's secretary for a final confirmation. The timeline was in her hands—along with my reputation. I emailed her a reminder two days before I needed the approval, which I thought was more than enough time. The deadline day arrived.

When I got into the office that morning, I waited (impatiently) until 8:30 for a response. Then I headed to her office to demand the information I needed. I intended to ask her why she hadn't gotten it to me already. After all, she was keeping me from completing my task at hand (and looking good in front of my superiors and peers). She was in the wrong.

I marched up the stairs, prepared to be firm with my boss's secretary. I knew the issue was the administrative staff's revolt against my changes, and I wasn't going to allow that to stand in the way of progress. When I reached her desk and asked about the invitation, she said she didn't have it done but hoped to have it to me by the end of the day.

I remember thinking, *Keep yourself composed.* My frustration level was rising.

Before I could form a verbal response, she said, "You know, Dawn, you are very controlling. If things aren't going just your way, you try to make everyone scramble to make it happen. You are not going to do that with me."

Did I get a taste of my own medicine that day or what? She put me right in my place. My need to control had prompted me to step on people instead of trying to relate to them. I had not taken into consideration any of her other responsibilities. I'd thought only about what I wanted and needed, and did what I could to get it, regardless of the cost.

Control Freaks Unite

I had bought in to the lie that I was in control. I believed I should do whatever it took to get the job done. Happily for me and everyone else around me, God has taught me how wrong that thinking is. *God* is in control. Period. Whatever control I feel I have or try to exert is due to my lack of faith in His abilities.

I doubt that I am the only control freak out there. I sense that there are others . . . maybe you. We want things to go our way, and we do all we can to make that happen. For some people, that means giving attention and diligence, but for an approval addict it easily becomes obsession and manipulation. We believe that we know the right thing to do and, if everyone would just listen to us, things would be a lot easier.

But approval addicts are prone to extremes that others are not. The healthiest thing for us is not having things go our way but remembering that we are not in control at all. Control is an illusion, a lie from the enemy. God alone is in control; He is sovereign. Things change when we let go, when we willingly and repeatedly surrender to Him and His control.

I would like to say it took only a tiny nudge from God and occasional reminders to help me understand and make changes in my attitudes and to align my behavior with God's Word. But that's not true. It took life-altering events for me to finally get the point.

The Turning Point

After three and a half years of marriage, my husband and I decided it was time for us to expand our family. Okay, the truth is that I am two years older than he is, and I wanted him to understand that it was time to get the baby-making process going. We prayed and asked God to confirm or correct us (or, more accurately, me). As our minds and spirits unified, we determined to move forward. I went off the pill and quickly became pregnant. But almost as soon as I read the positive pregnancy test, I began bleeding. I tested positive on Friday and lost our baby by Monday. We were devastated.

We took a few months to heal and pray, then decided it was time to try again. This time I didn't get pregnant quickly. Seven months later, just as we were thinking that maybe something was wrong, we learned I was pregnant.

I had changed jobs by this point and now worked for a software company that sold recruiting software to college admissions offices and trained them in using it. During my eighth week of pregnancy, I traveled from Ohio to Georgia for work.

I remember being excited that day. I had been having some mild pains, but I thought they were just early stages of implanting. That afternoon, I went to the bathroom and saw the blood. I was in the process of training my client, so I finished out my day, barely holding myself together. As soon as I could, I called my doctor. He suggested

I get a pregnancy test to know for sure whether I was miscarrying. I went to the local pharmacy. It didn't take long to know my worst fears were being realized again. I was in the process of miscarrying. The doctor then advised me to get home as soon as possible.

My boss concurred and told me to get on a plane home immediately. At eight weeks' pregnant, I flew from Atlanta to Cincinnati, barely able to speak to anyone through my hysteria. I had lost our baby in a stall of a women's restroom in the Atlanta airport. I am pretty sure everyone else in the restroom knew it, too.

From that moment, I was angry. Angry at God. Angry at the world. Angry at every teenager who had an unwanted pregnancy. I was angry with the drug addicts and prostitutes who were having children and giving them up for adoption. It wasn't fair. I loved God. I followed Jesus. Even though I had lived with my ex-husband prior to marriage, I was lost back then—it shouldn't count. After all, I didn't have sex before this marriage. Why did it feel like God was punishing me?

That December, while I continued walking through a fog of anger and bitterness, tragedy struck our Cincinnati church. During a performance of our annual Christmas pageant, one of the performers was belaying down from the ceiling and fell to her death. My husband was on staff and there that night. He still gets emotional during that portion of the show or any time he sees people performing on ropes or wires.

Our pastor asked the church to assemble—all ten thousand of us. He talked about the mourning process. It was not what I expected. It would have been easier for him to just talk around the issue, but he didn't. He was real and emotionally raw. We saw a side of him that night we had not seen before. I hadn't known the woman who died, but I did know loss. And as he spoke to an audience that was mourning a great loss, I finally began to work through my own.

The pastor shared a passage from the Bible book of Job: "Naked I came from my mother's womb, and naked shall I return. The LORD gave, and the LORD has taken away; blessed be the name of the LORD" (Job 1:21 ESV). He played a recording of Matt Redman's "Blessed Be the Name of the Lord," and explained how our hearts heal by letting go of our loved ones. Though the Lord gives, He also takes away. He does not owe us an explanation, though we can certainly ask.

Excuse me? God doesn't owe me an explanation?

The statement took me by surprise. I wanted to know—in fact, I had been demanding to know—what I had done wrong that God would deny me the chance to be a mother. I wanted nothing more than to become pregnant with our own child. I had wanted to be a mom since my sister was born when I was two and a half years old. Isn't God supposed to give us the desires of our hearts?

I received healing that night through the words of that pastor, through Matt Redman's song, and through the story of Job. Job was a blameless and upright man, blessed by God. Job hadn't done anything wrong. He wasn't causing problems; he wasn't worshiping other gods. In fact, Job was as close to perfect as a human could be, and for that very reason, he became Satan's target.

In what must have seemed like moments, all of Job's ten children and all his livestock were gone. One messenger after another came from far places to tell Job that his family, animals, and wealth had been destroyed. Can you even imagine being a parent and hearing that one child has died, let alone all ten on the same day? How broken would you be? Could you even manage a response at all?

Job did. Read his response again:

Then Job arose and tore his robe and shaved his head and fell on the ground and worshiped. And he said, "Naked I came from my mother's womb, and naked shall I return.

The Lord gave, and the Lord has taken away; blessed be the name of the Lord" (Job 1:20–21 ESV).

Did you catch that? *He worshiped God.* Every one of his children as well as his livestock were killed, and yet he worshiped the Lord. Somehow . . . somehow he turned his heart and voice toward God, saying, "He gives, and He takes away." Somehow Job chose to say, "Blessed be Your name."

Wow. Is it possible to make a conscious choice in the midst of our circumstances to say, "Lord, blessed be Your name"? To make a public confession of trust in God instead of our own wisdom and strength and timing? Our knee-jerk reaction is not to say, "blessed be Your name" but "why?" or even "how dare You?"

It does seem impossible because we think we should have control. God should answer to us. He owes us an explanation! But that is a lie, an illusion. We are *not* in control, and our rage and our tears when things don't happen the way we think they should show that we don't understand, accept, and believe the truth. And rather than blaming our lack of understanding, we blame Him. Rather than walking in the truth, we wallow in the lie. And our pain deepens and lengthens.

If you read to the end of Job's story, you see that God returned to him what was lost—more, in fact. Job's story teaches us how to respond when we realize that things are not in our control.

I can recall that Wednesday night as if it were happening right now. The room was completely dark, only a few dim lights were shining on the stage. The music played loudly in my ears, and my fists were clenched together. I remember thinking and saying to God, "I am so angry at You for miscarrying both of my babies. You put the desire in my heart to have children in the first place, why would You continue to take them away?" Then something in me broke, and I realized that regardless of the circumstances, I still loved my God. He had shown me so much grace, so much mercy, and so much kindness. It was only through His redemptive work in my life that I, a forgiven adulterer and divorcée, was standing there that night next to my husband, a man who loved the Lord and wanted to serve Him.

Slowly I lifted my fists above my head in surrender. I sang along with Matt Redman, tears streaming down my face. "He gives and takes away, but my heart will choose to say, blessed be the name of the Lord."

Whether I was ever to have a child or not, I would choose to praise Him. "Blessed be the name of the Lord."

Losing Control

It seemed like a hard lesson to learn during that season. I wish I could tell you that after that night I no longer felt the need to control things, people, or circumstances in my life. That's not the case, but that night made me realize the many things I did not control. I didn't control when my body could produce a child. I couldn't control the other women who were pregnant around me. I couldn't stop the jealousy I felt as I watched the babies grow inside them. I had no control over my need to please my parents or in-laws, my husband, or even my friends who so dearly wanted us to be able to become parents.

But there was one thing I knew I could control: whether I submitted to God and surrendered to His control. And I found that the more I chose His will over my plans, the more blessing and joy I experienced.

Later that month, friends invited us out to celebrate New Year's Eve at a posh restaurant in Cincinnati. On such occasions, I sometimes have a glass of wine. We were trying again to have a baby, so I decided to take a pregnancy test beforehand, just in case. I woke before my husband that morning and snuck into the bathroom. Those ten seconds felt like an eternity, and I snuck a quick look, long before the instructions said to. The line on the test turned bright blue! I nearly twisted my ankle running and leaping from the bathroom to share the news with my husband.

Eight months later, after a rocky pregnancy that ended with pre-eclampsia and an intense early labor, I gave birth to our beautiful baby boy. As I write this book, he is seven years old and the most incredible little being in my world. In him, God has given me constant reminders of His grace and His mercy. He is truly our miracle child.

Since his birth, we have lost three more babies. I could be a bitter person today, far from God because I didn't get my way. But I'm not, because of a December evening when I learned an important biblical truth: God is in control and I am not.

This truth is now woven throughout my life as God has taken us from Ohio to Alabama, moving us from our home to start a church that never took flight. He's allowed me to walk and grow through a serious virus, gallbladder surgery, and the removal of a carotid body tumor. I've struggled for years with a semi-diagnosed, long-term health condition that no one can seem to figure out. He keeps me on my toes today, teaching me to rely on Him in my home life, marriage, parenting, and my leadership position with our ministry at The Link. My motto over the years has become, "Live in obedience every day, so that He gets the glory."

That's essentially what Job was doing when he chose to praise God rather than focus on his tragic circumstances. I aspire to do the same. No matter what He gives or takes away, I will declare it: *Blessed be the name of the Lord.*

We cannot control what other people think of us. We cannot control the things that happen to us. We cannot control what someone else puts on Facebook or whether our friends have something we desire. We cannot control how our spouses respond or don't respond to us. We cannot control whether our children will love Jesus.

The truth is and always has been, *God is in control.* Period.

When you allow Him to do the work He does best as Creator and Ruler of the universe, you will be blessed. I am not saying it will be easy or that you will never hurt. The Bible does not promise such things. But we can know that we have a Father in heaven who loves us. If we choose to submit to Him and release our need for control, His name will be blessed—and so, increasingly, will our lives.

Lord God, You are sovereign and seated on Your throne. Nothing we go through is unseen or forgotten by You. You know it all. You see our hurts; You know our fears; You understand. You know the depths of pain we feel when we lose a loved one as You watched Your Son die on the cross. Your Word tells us that You give and You take away, but we are to say, "Blessed be the name of the Lord." To this we say in agreement, "Blessed be Your name."

Lord, You also know that our need to control others is directly correlated to our need for approval. I pray right now, God, that You would break those chains of reliance on human authority and approval and place in our hearts a desire for Your authority and approval. Help us walk in freedom by submitting to You daily, surrendering to Your control, and trusting and obeying You in everything we do, all for Your glory. In Jesus's name, amen.

Don't Take It So Personally

· · · · · · · · · ·

We don't think of ourselves as idolaters.
The idea seems so absurd.

BOB HOSTETLER

I'm glad social media did not exist when I was growing up. As an approval addict, I might not have survived my teenage years. I can only imagine how a negative tweet or post about me would have affected me. Or how my need for approval would have provoked me to post things I should have kept to myself. I'm sure I would not only have been offended and upset by posts about me, I would have read into things others posted and made them all about me whether they were directed at me or not.

Though social media came along after I reached adulthood, I have still had to learn not to take things personally; when I don't, I put *me* where *God* belongs—in the center of my world. I must be vigilant in preventing that from happening. I set boundaries for myself—I limit the time I spend online, and sometimes I go offline completely. It's easy to fall prey to me-centered thinking when I'm scrolling through a Twitter feed or a Facebook timeline. They invite comparisons and can breed negativity. If I'm not careful, before I know it, I'm grumpy, depressed, or even offended because I took something personally.

When we spend more time focusing on ourselves or something else than we do God, it is idolatry. In his book, *American Idols,* Bob Hostetler reminds us how easy it is to disobey God's commandment to place "no other gods before me" (Exodus 20:3). He writes,

> Generally speaking, none of us fall into idolatrous beliefs and behaviors intentionally—at least not at first. We don't set out to succumb to idolatry. We don't aspire to become idolaters. It's a subtle process, sinister even, imperceptible at first. It's a slow process, one that can take months or years to build.[14]

An addiction to approval, paired with the use of social media, can make us vulnerable to subtle (and some not-so-subtle) forms of idolatry. Before we know it, we've taken our eyes off God and made ourselves the center of attention.

Right before I started writing this book, an acquaintance of mine started spouting off on Facebook about me. I couldn't see all the drama because she blocked me, but other people within our circle of mutual friends starting commenting. These people weren't initially involved in the situation and didn't know the whole story (not that it was any of their business anyway).

My focus was completely on myself and my feelings. I was offended. I let my anger grow. I hosted a pity party for myself—table for one. I know that not everything that goes through my head should be posted online (or come out of my mouth), but I was sorely tempted to give in to my emotions and start replying, arguing with other people's posts. Instead, I held to what I know is true and kept my mouth shut—and my fingers still—in the midst of the drama.

That's all it really was: social media drama. The person posting was wounded. I had hurt her, and she wanted everyone to know it. The situation was becoming toxic, and instead of focusing on loving others, worshiping God, and doing what He called me to do, I was allowing myself to become a victim of the circumstances.

I had a choice to make. I could get further involved in the drama, whether in my own head or, worse, in my actions. Or I could choose to remove myself from the situation. I needed a way to defuse the situation. I prayed, which I've discovered is always a good decision. I felt the Lord asking me to completely refrain from using social media for thirty days. I obeyed, and found a new level of freedom and peace.

So much of what we struggle with is defined by what we're focused on. Focus determines priority. Consider this: how many times have you decided to diet and made eating healthy and exercising your focus? Maybe you researched a Couch-to-5k program, took a Zumba class, or found new recipes online and changed your grocery choices to support your new lifestyle. You kept that up for a while—ten days, a month, maybe even a few months. But before you knew it, old habits crept back in and you lost your focus. I know, I know; the struggle is real. I'm with you, all the way to the bread aisle.

The same thing can happen with our spiritual focus. We can be focused on God and His Word and all that He desires for us until suddenly, just like that, we see a squirrel and head off in a different direction. A me-focused direction.

The dictionary defines *focus* as "a state or condition permitting clear perception or understanding; an adjustment for distinct vision; the area that may be seen distinctly or resolved into a clear image."[15] It's the ability to see clearly. We can focus on ourselves and things others have done to us or against us, or we can focus on the One who can heal it all, the One whose Word tells us, "Look to the LORD and his strength; seek his face always" (1 Chronicles 16:11).

No Offense

Walking away from my online world for a season was the most liberating thing I had done in quite a while. Not only did I stop wondering who was talking about me and what they were saying, but I realized the other person no longer had the power to hurt and offend me. The freedom I experienced was amazing.

That experience taught me something I wish I had learned a long time ago. When I step away from the situation, focus my mind on God and His Word, and pray for my enemies, there's no longer room for me on the throne of my heart. And, if God's on that throne, I'm not nearly as likely to become offended.

The approval of others is important to an approval addict, and when we don't receive it, we often take offense. Our needs, feelings, and emotions become the center of our world. We're hurt, and the world is going to know it. But being offended also reveals our vulnerabilities, and we do not like that. Most of us don't want people to know that they've hurt us because that feels like they have won and we have lost. To protect ourselves, we hide our true emotions, such as sadness and even grief. The other person's behavior signals (to us) that they are not a friend or that they don't really like, love, or care for us. And that loss evokes a response of grief and sadness.

Instead of admitting and confronting our true emotions, we protect ourselves and defend our hearts by choosing to feel offended. This process is destructive because it keeps us focused on our wounds and ourselves. It elevates the wound and demands justice. The offender, however, cannot heal the wound. Even if that person asks for forgiveness, the fact of the wound still exists. If we forgive the other person, the fact of the wound still exists. Because it does, our focus remains on the wound and, thus, on ourselves. But the wound *can* be healed.

One of God's many names, *Jehovah Rapha*, is found in Exodus 15:26. The phrase means "The Lord your healer." It is not a title. It is not a description. It is a name. It refers to His character, the essence of who He is, and He cannot turn away from it. When your focus is on God rather than yourself and your hurt, then mourning, grieving, and crying in His presence become a cleansing baptism that brings about supernatural healing. You will never heal by focusing on the behavior of others or on the wounds they have caused. Healing comes by turning your eyes upon God.

You Have a Choice

Do you know someone who operates as if the whole world revolves around her (or him)? Someone who saps all your energy? Someone you constantly encourage and assure that they aren't as bad as they make themselves out to be? Someone you must repeatedly remind that all will be well and the world isn't ending over their current crisis?

I was that person. I needed people to validate me, constantly. I needed them to encourage me and lift me up. If they weren't saying kind or encouraging words about me, well then, I didn't want to listen. I took personally everything people said . . . and I was offended on a regular basis.

This mentality ruled my life for years. Then a friend taught me a powerful truth that stopped those toxic thoughts in their tracks. We were talking through a hurtful situation I'd experienced, when suddenly he said, "You know, Dawn, you can always choose not to be offended."

Wait, what? I can *choose* whether or not I'm offended? That's just crazy talk.

I thought offense was the natural response to people who hurt our feelings. Everyone does it. It's like squinting against the blazing sun. It's instinctual. Universal. Unavoidable. Right?

Remember the addiction approval cycle we talked about in Chapter 3? I suggested that the cycle begins when someone expresses a negative opinion about who we are or something we've done. We can choose to believe the person and take their words to heart, or we can choose not to take their words to heart. We can stop the cycle before it begins.

Dr. Henry Cloud, author of the book *Boundaries*, says, "We live in a society of people-pleasers and victims. People today act as if they have no choices in life and that everything should be done for them. If it's not, they can't do it themselves or make changes."[16]

Making the right choice is vital, from the start of a hurtful—or potentially hurtful—interaction. Otherwise we accept as fact that we're the victim, and we decide we can't change that fact; we must accept it, and other people should accept that fact about us as well. Except, once again, we've turned our focus on ourselves and our problems. We've forgotten to keep God in the center of the situation. We fixate on ourselves and our circumstances, when we should instead turn our eyes on God, worship Him alone, and allow Him to change our hearts and our circumstances.

Keep God in Focus

So, how do you change? How do you turn from a me-centered victim mentality to a focus that denies others the power or authority to dictate your moods and attitudes?

To begin the process, look at Jesus. He was adept at defusing His enemies' words in every situation. He interacted with every challenge the people brought Him without making the issue about Himself. Jesus didn't complain about what someone said about Him. He didn't do things just to please people. He never tried to gain the approval of the crowd. In fact, at times He seemed so elusive that His disciples questioned Him about it. No, Jesus always chose the right thing, the God-focused thing, rather than the thing that would please people.

Luke's Gospel records the story of Jesus in the wilderness, right after John baptized Him. This story can teach us how to overcome me-centered, offended thinking and instead remain focused on God. Luke 4:1–13 describes the forty days and forty nights during which Jesus fasted and prayed in the wilderness. The purpose of this time was to gain a razor-sharp focus on God. For those forty days Jesus "was tempted by the devil. He ate nothing during those days, and at the end of them he was hungry" (Luke 4:2).

This is one of my favorite lines in this story. After forty days of eating nothing and living in the wilderness, the man was hungry. Wow! Ya think? Of course, He was hungry—but Scripture points it out because it's important. Our flesh cries out for *something*, some need within us, and when that happens, it presents a prime opportunity for the devil to take advantage of us in our weakness.

The devil said to Jesus, "If you are the Son of God, tell this stone to become bread" (Luke 4:3). Jesus, at the end of His fast, must have known that He would soon eat, though He may have been miles from a good restaurant at that precise moment. It must have been tempting for Him to respond out of His hunger with me-centered, offended thinking: "I have gone without food for forty days. I think I've proved My point. What's a little food at this point going to matter? I am pretty much done. I mean, what's an hour or two in the grand scheme of things?"

Does that sound familiar at all? It's a line from the recording I play in my head when I'm fasting or on a diet. Right around the finish line, just as I'm about to experience the victory, my body wants to take a shortcut. Maybe this is why Paul urges us to "press on toward the goal to win the prize" (Philippians 3:14).

But our stubborn flesh pulls our focus from God to ourselves, to our needs, and more specifically, to our growling stomachs. Thankfully, Jesus responded differently than I would have; differently than you might have. He set an example for us to follow. Jesus answered, "It is written: 'Man shall not live on bread alone'" (Luke 4:4). Jesus could have easily turned a stone to bread. There is no doubt in my mind. He could turn water to wine, so of course He could make bread from a stone. The devil tempted Jesus with something Jesus was fully capable of doing, something His flesh would have been craving, even though He had put aside those forty days to seek the Father and not meet His physical needs.

The devil tempts us in the same way. He figures out what we crave most, and he uses that to turn our focus away from God and toward those desires. But Jesus didn't fall for it. He deflected. And He did it by using the Word of God. He quoted Deuteronomy 8:3, using it as ammunition against the devil's schemes.

Next the devil tried to attack Jesus's ego. "The devil led him up to a high place and showed him in an instant all the kingdoms of the world. And he said to him, 'I will give you all their authority and splendor; it has been given to me, and I can give it to anyone I want to. If you worship me, it will all be yours'" (Luke 4:5–7). This was Satan's second attempt to get Jesus's focus off the Father and onto Himself and His desires. This temptation was another shortcut. After forty days in the wilderness, Jesus knew that His ordeal had just begun. He faced a long and grueling period of ministry and sacrifice before His exaltation. So, the devil gave Jesus a chance to bypass it all.

But Jesus knew where His authority came from: "It is written: 'Worship the Lord your God and serve him only'" (Luke 4:8).

Jesus again deflected the enemy's attack by using the Word of God. He deliberately took the focus off Himself and placed it on God, where it belonged. Our focus always belongs on God, and authority always rests with Him.

Finally, the devil tempted Jesus to question His identity as the Son of God and to test whether the Father was with Him by forcing the Father's hand.[17] Luke 4:9–11 continues:

> The devil led [Jesus] to Jerusalem and had him stand on the highest point of the temple. "If you are the Son of God," he said, "throw yourself down from here. For it is written: 'He will command his angels concerning you to guard you carefully; they will lift you up in their hands, so that you will not strike your foot against a stone.'"

In other words, "If Your Father really cares, He will take care of You. Try Him . . . see what happens." The suggestion was, if the Father didn't do what Jesus asked, than He didn't really care about Jesus.

Sound familiar? Believing this lie is detrimental to your relationship with the Lord. Believe it, and before you know it, you're questioning everything. *Does He really love me? Does He care? How could He have allowed that to happen to me?* It changes the whole relationship because you lose trust in God, and instead you begin thinking you must take matters into your own hands, that you are the ruler of your own universe, and that, since He doesn't care and won't come through for you, you need to handle this situation—every situation—on your own.

But how did Jesus respond? The same way He did to the other

temptations—with a razor-sharp focus and wisdom from the Word of God. Jesus answered, "It is said: 'Do not put the Lord your God to the test'" (Luke 4:12). Rather than allowing the devil to shift His attention, Jesus repeatedly turned Himself back to the proper focus, saying essentially, "You can tempt Me all you want, but the Father is My focus."

None of this is any different for us. No, the devil won't tempt you to turn stones into bread, but he'll find something that appeals to you. Temptations will always be there. They come in three forms:

1. the temptation to worry about the provision of your human needs;
2. the temptation to choose your plans and your timeline over the Father's plans and timing; and
3. the temptation to question who you are and whether God cares, is listening, and really understands.

These temptations, should you fall prey to them, will take your focus from God and place it on you, making you believe you are or need to be in control of your situation. But as we discussed in Chapter 4, you are not in control, and all efforts to look or feel like you are will only complicate things and increase your frustration.

Jesus could have allowed His circumstances to change His focus. He could have chosen to prioritize *His* needs, *His* desires, *His* plans. But instead, Jesus warded off the attacks of the enemy by putting the focus on God—and He used Scripture as His weapon.

How about you? Have you been tempted in any of these ways? If so, did you respond as Jesus did, with Scripture as your weapon of choice? If you're anything like me, the answer is probably no. Unlike Jesus, we don't always recognize the source of our temptations, that it is Satan who is speaking to us. We don't see the real picture and don't easily turn to Scripture, as we should.

You are not a victim of your circumstances. You may have presented a bull's-eye for the enemy's attacks, but that does not mean the arrow has to stick. In fact, Ephesians 6:16 tells us that we can put on the shield of faith and thus deter the flaming arrows of the evil one. You don't have to respond the same way you always have. You can choose *not* to be offended by the things someone says to you. You don't have to make it all about you. You can choose to learn the Word of God, and you can use it against the enemy. You can learn who you are in Christ and stand firm in who God created you to be. You can choose to live as a victor rather than a victim.

If we would choose to use Scripture as our weapon and learn how to turn our focus more sharply on God when tempted, our perceptions would change—especially our perceptions of other people and how we respond to them. We would be better able to empathize with their wounds and not fixate on our own wounds in response. We would desire to experience the pleasure of God and not worry about pleasing others. We would walk in more freedom and less bondage to our own needs.

Don't you want more of that? I know I do. So let's go hard after God, let's seek Him and not allow every situation we walk into to become all about us. Let's not take things personally; instead, let's place our hurts, pains, and temptations in the hands of the One who is truly in control of it all.

Jesus, we love You so much. Thank You for the example of Your life on earth. In it we can see Your desire to empathize with us. Thank You that, as the Word says, "we do not have a high priest who is unable to empathize with our weaknesses, but we have one who has been tempted in every way, just as we are—yet he did not sin" (Hebrews 4:15). You know our hurts, You understand our pain, and You know the need we feel to have the approval of those around us. Help us not to take offense and nurse our wounds, but to seek You and focus on You, remembering always that our battles are not against flesh and blood, but rather against the powers of darkness. You are our defender. You go before us and fight for us. We "need only to be still" (Exodus 14:14).

Community versus Comparison

- - - - - - - - - - -

We won't be distracted by comparison
if we are captivated by purpose.

BOB GOFF

Community. It's such a great word. I love the way it sounds and the ideas it conjures in my head. The word evokes memories of people I have done life with through some exciting and trying times. It gives me a sense of belonging and allows me to be part of something bigger than myself. Community draws me into relationship with other people and keeps me from isolation.

Over my lifetime, I have moved nearly thirty times, living in nine cities in four different states. I've experienced communities of all shapes and sizes and have traveled throughout the country and abroad. Yet my favorite places to live have always been those small- to medium-sized cities that provide access to the necessities of life—

you know, things like coffee, sushi, and bookstores. I like the feel of a place where people know who you are.

That pretty much sums up my life in Cullman, Alabama. Cullman is a growing city. In the past five years, we've gone from one Walmart to two and added a Panera, a Dick's Sporting Goods, and a Ross. Everything in town is within a fifteen-minute drive. There aren't many places I go that I don't run into someone I know and end up in a twenty-minute conversation, even though we probably saw each other earlier in the week. In this little town, being in a hurry is never an excuse to pass by a friend or acquaintance without at least a quick hello. It slows down the grocery shopping, but I love it.

I feel safe and secure in a place where I am known, and I know the people around me. I like the predictability of small-town life. I might enjoy visiting a city with hundreds of thousands of people (mostly strangers), but it is not where I want to put down roots.

I've joined a new type of community in the last few years—the online community. As I get to know my friends and followers there, my online communities feel increasingly small and comfortable. At the same time, they grow progressively larger as I connect with people who live in other cities and states, and even other countries. Social media has drastically changed the way we become part of a community, faster and more comprehensively than at any other time in history. In moments, the world can feel ten times smaller because you can access information from anyone, anywhere.

We can interact with each other through blogging, Facebook, Instagram, Pinterest, YouTube, Snapchat, and Periscope, to name only a few. New products pop up every day, giving us more cutting-edge ways to engage with others. People have built entire companies and causes on their online community platforms alone.

Online communities can benefit many types of organizations, from business owners and entrepreneurs to charitable organizations, schools, churches, and sports teams. Whatever your interest, you can probably find a group or an app online related to that activity or interest.

Mark Zuckerberg, the creator of Facebook, says,

When I made Facebook . . . my goal was to help people understand what was going on in their world a little better. I wanted to create an environment where people could share whatever information they wanted, but also have control over whom they shared that information with. I think a lot of the success we've seen is because of these basic principles.[18]

As much as I love to scroll through my Facebook or Instagram feeds, however, my favorite way to engage in community is in person—whether one-on-one or in a small group. This is especially true when those people are like me in their love for Jesus and when they challenge me to learn more about Him in new and fresh ways. Few things are more encouraging, empowering, or helpful than being part of a group like that.

What's in Your Heart?

But what happens when communities are not healthy? What happens when things that were meant for good turn bad? And what if you are part of the reason your community is unhealthy? What if you and your need for approval negatively affect the people around you? What if, instead of your online communities being places where you are cheering others on, encouraging them, and lifting them up, you are comparing yourself with others and destroying any chance at a healthy, loving relationship?

That is the adverse affect an approval addict can have in a community. I wish I could say this was unfamiliar territory to me. It would be so much easier to write this if I could say I've conquered the issue, but my struggles in this area are more apparent to me today than ever before. But this is a good thing. I can more easily and quickly identify jealousy and envy in myself. I'm no longer blind to my own weakness in this area—and that awareness makes me stronger.

I look back now and realize how horribly I've behaved toward some of the women in my life. If my thoughts had been actions, I would have torn many a woman to shreds. I was stuck in a rut of comparison. Comparing hairstyles. Clothing. Body types. Personality. Intelligence. You name it, I have probably compared it. Christian or not, it didn't matter. I rationalized my thinking, coaxing myself into believing my comparisons were okay, that I was okay.

As a wife, my behavior was worse and my rationalizations stronger. "A wife should be jealous over her husband the way God is over us" was my excuse on most occasions. There is truth in that statement, but I used it to justify my insecurity and imagination. I ended up tearing down rather than building up our friends. I cringe to think how many women I belittled or isolated from us as a couple through my words or behavior.

But community is so much more important than comparison. As the leader of a ministry called The Link of Cullman County, you might think unity and community would come easy for me. But the devil has a counterfeit for every good and perfect creation of God—including God's vision to unify the body of Christ by meeting the needs of the poor. The devil is divisive and will do whatever he can to divide and conquer. I sought unity in my community, even as the enemy stirred up the dissension in my heart that kept me in bondage to jealousy and envy.

When I first started the ministry, I was jealous of everything and everyone. I was jealous of the established nonprofits that seemed to easily raise funds. I was jealous of leaders who, because of their earned respect in the community, were asked to speak at civic groups or churches. I was jealous of their long experience, grumbling because I had to work so much harder (I thought) to learn this new calling God had placed on my life. I felt constantly disadvantaged because I was doing nearly everything by trial and error—mostly error.

I did my best to suppress those feelings because—seriously, I led an organization whose mission was all about working together, partnering, supporting one another, and not competing. But I had a dark secret in my heart. Jealousy was ruling me, and competition was driving me.

It didn't help that my peers were not happy with the new kid on the nonprofit block. I was another competitor, going after dollars in a small town. Our arrival on the nonprofit scene had engendered fear, I was told, in the other executive directors' minds because donors liked new, shiny things, and their organizations had been around for a while. Their jealousy only had me fighting harder and comparing my every move to them, wondering what they would do next.

All along, God knew my people-pleasing tendencies. He knew my jealous heart. He knew how badly I believed I needed a yes as I went out and spoke to potential donors and community partners. He knew the secrets I could not hide. It didn't take long before I began feeling a check in my spirit. Perhaps you've experienced this— a warning from the Holy Spirit. Sometimes it's a nudge; sometimes it's like a bodycheck in a fierce hockey game. Maybe you didn't realize at first that your heart was in the wrong place, but now you know you are out of line. When that happens, you can choose to repent and receive forgiveness and healing, or you can keep moving in your own direction, ignoring the Holy Spirit and paying the consequences.

I ignored the Spirit as long as I could. I justified my response to the other leaders because it felt like they were against me. I talked my way around my inner thoughts because, if I said I believed in unity, then surely it would come true. But God used an online community to show me my wrong thinking and teach me that I wasn't really "for" the other groups in my community, no matter how hard I tried to convince myself or others that I was.

I'd been following a variety of different women entrepreneurs on Instagram. They inspired me. I loved to watch what they were creating and promoting. These women were all starting businesses, mostly out of their own homes. They were go-getters, creative people who had vision and direction. It was hard not to be jealous of their talents.

If you were checking out Instagram during this period, you would have seen intense competition. People were appropriating ideas and calling them their own. Nothing seemed sacred. I am sure these women held their ideas close for fear someone else would steal them and beat them to production and sales. I saw many angry posts from women who were trying to share new creations, only to find out that someone else had swooped in and copied their ideas.

At the same time, however, I noticed another theme running through some of the posts. It was identified with the hashtag: #communityovercompetition. "Wow!" I thought. "That's inspiring." I loved the idea of cheering each other on, of encouraging another femalepreneur to do her best in whatever she was doing. It was refreshing, and I wanted to be a part of it.

It made me realize, however, that I needed to take a long, hard look at my own heart. I had to consider my role in my community and how I responded to fellow nonprofit/ministry leaders in pursuit of their calling. Was I lifting them up or tearing them down? Was I cheering them on or backbiting them? Was I supporting or undermining them?

As you can imagine, it didn't take long for the Lord to reveal to me the darkness that had seeped into my heart. I was not building community; I was destroying it. My need for the approval of people around me, to be viewed as successful, trumped my willingness to cheer on and champion other causes that mattered in my community. I was humbled and disappointed in myself.

I had believed the lie that I had value only if I was the brightest star and the most recognized voice in my community. That's what comparison does—it breaks down the walls of kindness and encouragement and builds up barriers of division and defeat. God's design is for us is to experience unity in community, but unity cannot exist in a place where comparison runs unchecked.

Unity of the Spirit

The essence of the word *community* is "a unified body of individuals."[19] But the dictionary is not the only place we find the idea of unity in relation to community.

Paul spoke to the Ephesians about this ideal, instructing them about God's plan for community. He explained that God's plan was for unity in the body of Christ, the church. God's desire was that they would honor each other in the context of community by putting Christ above all things. In Ephesians 4:1–6 ESV, Paul wrote:

I therefore, a prisoner for the Lord, urge you to walk in a manner worthy of the calling to which you have been called, with all humility and gentleness, with patience, bearing with one another in love, eager to maintain the unity of the Spirit in the bond of peace. There is one body and one Spirit— just as you were called to the one hope that belongs to your call—one Lord, one faith, one baptism, one God and Father of all, who is over all and through all and in all.

We have so much to learn from these words. In the first verse, Paul reveals how he sees himself and his role in the kingdom. He refers to himself as a "prisoner for the Lord." This was literally true; he wrote these words as a prisoner under guard in Rome. But he also considered himself a prisoner in his calling as a minister of the gospel. As such, Paul chooses to focus, not on his poor circumstances, but rather on the freedom and calling placed upon him by the Lord—and he encourages the Ephesians to do the same. Each of us—you and I—have the same calling and the same responsibility. And the community or communities that we are a part of are included in that calling.

Do you see Paul encouraging community or comparison in these verses? There is nothing here to suggest that Paul wants us to compare our lives with someone else's life. He doesn't even suggest that we should compare our situation to his. In fact, he says that when we conduct ourselves in a manner worthy of our calling, we are doing the exact opposite—we'll see ourselves as valued, important, significant, and unique. We can walk with our heads held high, not because we are proud but because we are secure in the calling God has placed on our lives.

This becomes even clearer as Paul explains what our lives should look like: We should be humble, gentle, and full of patience. We should bear with one another in love, and eagerly maintain the unity of the Spirit in the bond of peace. We're not to be consumed with what everyone else is doing. We shouldn't strive to live like the Joneses or compete with our neighbors. We must stop because it's coveting, plain and simple. And coveting is sin.

Does any of this describe you? Are you eager to maintain the unity of the Spirit? Are you anxious and willing to lay aside the comparison that creates division and dissension and seek out honest community that unifies the spirits of all involved?

Paul says we are called to be one body—there is one Spirit, one hope, one Lord, one faith, one baptism, and one God who is Father over all. He intentionally repeats that three-letter word, "one."

This the essence of community. Do we see ourselves as one body? Does our behavior reflect the control of one Spirit? Do we act as though we all share one hope? Do we rejoice that we are all one faith? Do we conduct ourselves as those who have been cleansed by the same baptism? Whose Father is the same God?

As Christ-followers, you and I have some serious heart-checking to do. It's time to decide if we truly believe the Word of God and are willing to do what it says.

Recovering approval addicts must recognize and acknowledge every day that comparison will divide the church. Comparison harms our "one body." When we compare ourselves to one another, we figuratively tear ourselves limb from limb; we break down and destroy those whom Christ came to save. In the name of Jesus Christ, we need to stop. We must stop scanning social media to see what someone else is doing, wearing, or driving. We must stop striving to be like, look like, act like, and feel like others.

We must instead do what Paul has told the Ephesians. We must live in a manner worthy of our calling. Our lives should radiate and demonstrate humility, gentleness, and patience as we bear with one another in love, eager to maintain the unity of the Spirit in the bond of peace.

How do we do that? Only through God's empowering Spirit. The only way I can tame the comparison monster who likes to rise up within me is through reliance on God. When I choose to pray about the person or thing I would otherwise compare myself to, my heart changes, and I shift from comparison to community. When I begin to feel jealous because another organization has received a large sum of money, I now choose to thank God for the people who will be served through the gift. I thank Him for answering prayers for their organization's needs. If I know the CEO or director, I will text or contact that person and congratulate them. By doing so, I submit myself to the authority of God, reminding myself that He is the provider of all things. I remember that He engineers the good of those who are called according to His purpose (Romans 8:28).

When I hear about a woman who is experiencing something wonderful, instead of thinking "no fair" or "why not me" or any other destructive thought, I start praying for her. I thank God for her life, friendship, and calling. I lift her up in prayer and cheer her on in the Spirit. If I know her and can reach out, I encourage her verbally as well. In doing so, I am loving her, and I am demonstrating my eagerness to maintain the unity of the Spirit in the bond of peace.

These are lessons I have learned after years of tearing people down in my mind and sometimes with my mouth. This path has not been easy for me, and I have been convicted more often of my wrongdoing than I have managed to live out the truth. But I promise you—if we can get our heads around the value and importance of biblical community in our lives, instead of comparing ourselves to everyone and everything around us, we will walk in a level of freedom we have never before experienced.

So join me. Agree with me in the Spirit to stop comparing yourself online and in person with those around you. Cultivate an eagerness to maintain unity while living in humility, gentleness, and patience toward others. Choose to encourage and cheer on your neighbors by bearing with them in love. Then the world will see exactly what Christ had in mind for us as the church, His bride—that we be as one body, led by one Spirit, expressing and reflecting one hope.

Jesus, our hearts are broken today by the reality of our destructive ways. We as Your church repent for the ways in which we have torn each other down through comparison when we should have been building each other up in community. From this day forward, we will seek to live in a manner worthy of the calling that You have called us to. We will respond in humility, gentleness, and patience, bearing with one another in love. We will be eager to achieve and maintain the unity of the Spirit through the bond of peace. We want the world to see Your church as one body, led by one Spirit, expressing and reflecting one hope. Help us to cheer each other on, to pray for each other's successes, and to get excited over what You are doing in our friends' lives, knowing that Your provision is enough. We want to be people who seek community over comparison in all we do. We ask this in Your holy and precious name, amen.

That Chip on Your Shoulder

· · · · · · · · · · ·

Insanity is doing the same thing over and over
again expecting different results.

UNKNOWN

I didn't mean to do it. Not really. I had no idea I was causing so much damage to my marriage and such pain to my husband. But I was frustrated because, in my opinion, he was not meeting my needs. Years of arguing over the same issues caused distance between us, and the distance felt heavy in the room that day. We found ourselves in another heated argument, and we were getting nowhere.

The discussion began calmly enough. I was sharing my concerns over his insensitivity about helping me around the house. I focused on dishwashing. I had kept score of the number of times I had done the dishes that week, and the number was in the double digits. I also placed a big fat zero in his column.

My husband explained why he had not done the dishes (they felt like excuses to me) and explained that he had helped in other ways. So I demanded a list of what he had done—and when. (Oh, yes, I did!) He, now visibly irritated with me, mentioned how busy he had been, which only aggravated me more, since I knew before the conversation began that my schedule had eclipsed his. Are you with me yet, or am I the only woman on the planet to have this kind of conversation? Something tells me I'm not.

Have you ever cornered another person with unassailable arguments because that person was not living up to your expectations? I wish I could say I have only had these conversations with my husband, but I can't. I am a perfectionist, especially when it comes to what I believe *other* people should be doing. Most of the time, I don't bother to consider whether I have verbally and accurately communicated those expectations, either. My ridiculous and inflated expectations that other people should live up to my standards (which I don't always reach myself) have caused friction in a variety of my relationships.

The scene with my husband was not new, of course. We'd followed this pattern for years. I kept a running list of expectations, spoken and unspoken. If he tried to bring up an area in which I had fallen short, I would quickly counter with my list of his failures. The discussion would get heated, and one of us would walk away. Eventually we'd both cool down enough to make apologies. Unfortunately, that never took us to a resolution, only to a truce.

Instead of giving and experiencing true forgiveness, we engaged in verbal battles from which one person walked away in bitter victory, and both of us nursed our wounds. The wounds festered. Sometimes they scabbed over; sometimes they became infected. Often they were reopened by a new skirmish in an old dispute.

Cycles like these never help a situation. When we feel like the victim, we don't see any reason to change. To a victim, the solution is always in someone else's hands.

But most often, the reality of the situation is that both persons are at fault. It isn't long before we're carrying chips on our shoulders. Chips can get heavy. They redefine who we are. They remind us of the last time we were at this pass and how nothing has changed since then. They drip with self-justification—we have done so much more in the relationship than the other person; we've made strides forward, and the other person has not.

A chip on the shoulder destroys relationships slowly and methodically. It's a main component of the approval cycle we looked at in Chapter 3, which is repeated on the following page. It shows up after someone has identified an area of insecurity for us, and we're feeling shame or guilt over what they've pointed out. It leads us to distance ourselves from people and encourages us to look at others' flaws. We nurse our anger and bitterness, deflecting our wrong and magnifying theirs. Whether in a marriage, friendship, or coworker situation, this part of the cycle can degrade and destroy even the strongest relationship.

Few of us do it intentionally. I don't know many people who lay out expectations while hoping the other person can't achieve them. In fact, I think it's the opposite. Most of our expectations point to things that would makes us feel honored and loved by the other person, so when they don't behave or respond as we hope, we feel hurt and anger.

If we look more closely at the root of our anger, we'll see approval needs oozing all around it. When someone doesn't perform the way we want and expect them to, we perceive it as disinterest in us and our needs. We allow it to devalue our relationship. In my case, when my husband pointed out my inability to fulfill his needs, I felt like less of a wife. My knee-jerk response was to deflect and place

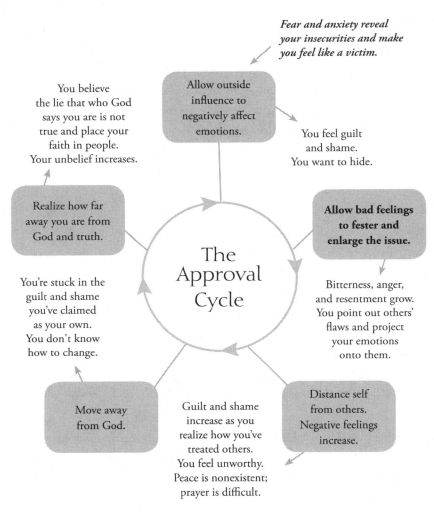

Fear and anxiety reveal your insecurities and make you feel like a victim.

Allow outside influence to negatively affect emotions.

You feel guilt and shame. You want to hide.

You believe the lie that who God says you are is not true and place your faith in people. Your unbelief increases.

Realize how far away you are from God and truth.

The Approval Cycle

Allow bad feelings to fester and enlarge the issue.

Bitterness, anger, and resentment grow. You point out others' flaws and project your emotions onto them.

You're stuck in the guilt and shame you've claimed as your own. You don't know how to change.

Move away from God.

Guilt and shame increase as you realize how you've treated others. You feel unworthy. Peace is nonexistent; prayer is difficult.

Distance self from others. Negative feelings increase.

the blame on him. His requests felt overwhelming and unrealistic; I felt like I could never live up to them. And though I didn't know it, he felt the same way. It wasn't until he explained it to me that I realized how wrong I was. In trying to cover up my insecurities, I would throw back at him *all* the ways I believed he had failed me as a husband—not just household chores, but anything I could think of to minimize my weaknesses and magnify his shortcomings.

Suddenly I realized how much damage had been done in our marriage. We had moved far away from the freedom and health we'd enjoyed in the early years. Our need for approval from one another had taken a toll. Our anger had caused unforgiveness. Unforgiveness had become bitterness. . . . It was a downward spiral that kept us from experiencing the freedom provided for us through Jesus's death on the cross. It also prevented us from experiencing a healthy relationship where we could be the people God had created us to be. It was unfair and unrealistic on both of our parts. We were both wrong.

Something had to change. Some*one* had to change. I already knew that nagging my husband wouldn't work. I knew that expressing my frustration only frustrated him.

I had a choice to make. I could hope and expect and wait for him to change, or I could ask God to change my own heart. It didn't take long, once I started praying for wisdom, for the Lord to reveal to me the antidote to our struggles.

First, He showed me my negative thought patterns. The lie of self-justification was at the top of the list. I believed that my anger was justified because my husband was not living up to the role I thought he should fulfill. Next, I had also fallen into unbelief. Years of feeling like nothing was changing had me believing the lie that God could not or would not fix this situation, so I needed to take matters into my own hands. Lastly, I had chosen to take up an offense against my husband. Anything he said to defend himself threw fuel on my already raging fire of bitterness. There was little he could do to put it out. All of this was destructive. I was spinning out of control, stuck in an approval-addiction cycle that was destroying my marriage.

Does this story bring a situation or relationship in your life to mind? Disputes like this don't just happen in marriage. Maybe you've experienced a similar situation in a family relationship, a friendship, or with a coworker. You know the relationship has grown toxic, but you can't figure out how to change it. Maybe at this point, you're just avoiding conflict by refusing to address the issue. Maybe you're so hurt and angry over unmet expectations that you've stopped pursuing the relationship completely. But difficult situations must be dealt with. Gritting your teeth and exercising your willpower will not accomplish much.

Regardless of the other person's response, we must remember that we ourselves have fallen far short of God's standards, yet He shows us unfailing mercy. And because of His mercy, we should show mercy and grace to others. It's not easy to do on our own. In fact, the only way we can learn to change our response is by asking God to renew our minds through His Word.

The story of Jonah in the Bible is a good place to start.

God told the prophet Jonah to go to Nineveh, a wicked Assyrian city (Jonah 1:2), to tell them about God and the destruction the people would soon face if they did not repent of their wickedness. Jonah had other thoughts on the matter, so instead of going to Nineveh, he got on a boat headed to Tarshish, in the opposite direction from Nineveh. But God pursued him with a huge storm. Eventually, Jonah told the boat's crew to save themselves by throwing him overboard. They did, and he was swallowed by a large fish. While in the belly of the fish, Jonah repented and the fish vomited him up onto the shore. (Gross, right?)

Still reluctant but not wanting to disobey God any further, Jonah went to Nineveh and shared the message God had given him. And the worst thing happened—the king and all his people repented and turned to God. Jonah 3:10 NASB says, "When God saw their deeds, that they turned from their wicked way, then God relented concerning the calamity which He had declared He would bring upon them. And He did not do it."

Jonah's response to this? "But it greatly displeased Jonah and he became angry." (Jonah 4:1 NASB). Now, you may think, "What? How could he? He was a prophet of God!" But Nineveh was not some random city; it was part of Assyria, and the Assyrians were enemies. And they were not nice people. Jonah knew about the wickedness that happened in Nineveh and by the hands of the Ninevites. He'd grown up hearing another prophet, Nahum, preach against the wicked city and prophesy its fall. Nahum 3:1–7 describes the sins of this city, including temple prostitution, child sacrifice, abortion, and infanticide. They were notorious for tearing off the ears and noses of their prisoners and then turning them out into the city to put fear into the hearts of the people. They were the ISIS of their day, yet they repented, and God granted them grace rather than wrath.

This did not make Jonah happy. In fact, he was so upset that the enemies of his people had escaped punishment that he stomped out of the city to sulk in the blazing sun. Jonah threw a tantrum because God didn't do what Jonah wanted Him to do. He protested and, in Jonah 4:2–3 NASB, prayed:

"Please LORD, was not this what I said while I was still in my own country? Therefore in order to forestall this I fled to Tarshish, for I knew that You are a gracious and compassionate God, slow to anger and abundant in lovingkindness, and one who relents concerning calamity. Therefore now, O LORD, please take my life from me, for death is better to me than life."

In other words, "I knew You were going to do this. I told You I didn't want You to do this to *these* people. You know what? To remedy this and my heart, just kill me."

But God answered, "Do you have good reason to be angry?" (Jonah 4:4 NASB).

Ouch! Do you hear that jab at Jonah's ego? Jonah registered his outrage with God, and God said, "I'm sorry, what are *you* angry about?"

I ask you the same thing today. Think about the situation that's formed that chip on your shoulder. Think about the person you keep butting heads with because they're not doing what you want. And consider your feelings toward God in this situation.

Do you have good reason to be angry? Or are you like Jonah, frustrated because God has not delivered the judgment you think someone else deserves? Is it because their hearts have not changed the way you think they should have changed? Or could it possibly be that you are so addicted to approval that when others fail to respond as you think they should, you throw a tantrum of your own?

Hey, I'm right there with you. This pity party is not just for one. In fact, it's so crowded in here that we're bumping into each other and maybe harming each other by being a part of it. We feed off each other's frustrations because we relate all too well. And in doing so, we are sinning and distancing ourselves from God's grace.

So what do we do? Look back at Jonah's example. In chapter 4, verse 2, Jonah tells us exactly who God is and teaches us how to respond to the person we directed our anger toward. "You are a gracious and compassionate God," he says. "Slow to anger and abundant in lovingkindness." Since this is who our God is and how He acts toward humanity—including ourselves—don't you think we should exhibit those same traits to those around us?

First, we need to be *gracious*, which is defined by the freely given, unmerited favor of God. If He offers grace freely, not asking us to earn it in any way, should we not also extend grace to those around us? Even those who do not live up to our expectations? Remember, it was God's grace that brought the Ninevites to repentance. If God's grace can accomplish that for you and for the Ninevites, don't you think He could also achieve it for others in your life?

We must also be *compassionate*. We are to feel deep sympathy and sorrow for those who are stricken by misfortune, and that empathy should be accompanied by a strong desire to alleviate the suffering.[20] For me, showing compassion is harder at times than showing grace. I have to work hard at it. My tendency is to demand justice when I feel wronged. When I am at my wits' end with my husband for not doing the things I have asked or expected him to do, I am as far from compassion as I can get. I don't want to make the situation better for him. I want the situation to be better for me. And in that position, I become the person causing his suffering—the opposite of compassion, and the polar opposite of the likeness of God.

Which brings us to the next character trait we should emulate: being *slow to anger*. The word *slow* in this phrase means long, as in being longsuffering or patient. Longsuffering could be described as being so slow and drawn out that it causes suffering to ourselves before we allow the anger to be displayed to another.

How patient has God been with you? How many flaws and failings has He put up with from you? How many times do you suppose He has had reason to respond in anger to your actions, but has been patient with you instead? We are to become like Him and respond in the same way to others.

Jonah also says that God is abundant in *lovingkindness*. It's a unique word. It indicates kindness, mercy, goodness, faithfulness, love, and acts of kindness.[21] Our reactions to others, whether they meet our expectations or not, should reflect kindness, mercy, faithfulness to our relationship, and above all else, love.

The last thing Jonah says about God's character in verse 2 is that He relents from sending calamity. The word *relent* in Hebrew is *nâcham*. It means to be sorry for, to pity, to console, to comfort, or to avenge.[22] In context, it is clear what Jonah means: God had pity on the Ninevites and saved them from calamity.

What an incredibly beautiful picture of who God is and how unlike Him we are when we respond with anger, frustration, or impatience when we don't get our way. Just like He did with Jonah, God uses these Ninevite moments to remind us of who we are, considering who He is. He grants us a choice when He asks, "Do you have good reason to be angry?"

I hope by now you are as convicted as I was (and still am today) over my inability to align my thinking and behavior to God's nature. Do I have good reason to be angry? No. I have no good reason to be angry with my God, my Abba Father. Nor do I have reason to be angry with my spouse or any other person who is not living up to my expectations. Because when I take a step back and realize all the mercy and grace God has shown toward me, I realize how wrong I have been.

Now, please understand—there are times when godly anger is an appropriate response to the injustices happening around us. Matthew 21 recounts how Jesus threw over the tables in the temple when He learned the people were using His Father's house for money-making rather than for worship. He was outraged by the injustice He witnessed. You, too, can become outraged by the injustices of the world, but let that outrage move you to a place of compassion for those who are being oppressed, enslaved, or abused. God wants you to be involved in these injustices. If He didn't, He wouldn't have had the prophet Micah declare, "The LORD has told you what is good, and this is what he requires of you: to do what is right, to love mercy, and to walk humbly with your God" (Micah 6:8 NLT).

We must strive to be full of grace, to be willing to have compassion, and to be slow to anger and abundant in lovingkindness. We must model these characteristics to our children, friends, family, and coworkers. This is how they will repent and be saved or obtain healing or feel loved. And as it was with Nineveh, when they repent, God will relent and, though they may suffer some natural consequences of their actions, they will experience the deliverance Jesus's death on the cross provides.

So this is your choice today: You can be a woman who chooses to be angry every time someone doesn't do as you ask, or you can be a woman who is full of grace, compassion, and lovingkindness, one who is slow to anger and relents concerning calamity. Which will you choose?

Lord God, You are a gracious, compassionate God who is slow to anger, abundant in lovingkindness, and more than willing to relent in sending calamity. I am not yet that kind of person—but I want to be. Forgive me for my temper, forgive me for holding people in my life to a different standard than I hold myself, and forgive me for not showing others the compassion and mercy You have shown to me. Change my heart, Lord; make me new. Teach me through the conviction of the Holy Spirit to show grace to others as You have shown me grace. Teach me to take on the suffering of others and be willing to walk with them in the compassion You have shown to me. Teach me how to be patient in my anger, not allowing it to consume me quickly. Rather help me show others the lovingkindness You have shown me. Give me eyes to look upon the wickedness of people with sorrow, realizing their distance from You. Only through the Holy Spirit and the sanctification of my heart can I do these things. I trust You, Lord, to renew my mind through Your Word. In Jesus's name, amen.

Rejected!

• • • • • • • • • •

Most fears of rejection rest on the desire
for approval from other people.
Don't base your self-esteem on their opinions.

HARVEY MACKAY

I created a noncontroversial Facebook post asking people to share their thoughts on something I had been pondering. I was looking for feedback. I posted in the middle of the day and waited. And waited. And waited. No one liked, commented, or shared my post. Not a single person. I felt completely rejected and started to wonder if I had any true friends at all. It was horrible.

Has this happened to you? You put yourself out there in some way on social media, and you were flat-out rejected. Maybe you heard nothing but crickets instead of the encouragement you expected from your friends. Or maybe you shared your heart and received an onslaught of negative responses. Maybe no one understood why you posted what you did? Maybe they read into your post something you did not say.

Social media has intensified our tendency to feel rejected. Prior to the age of the internet, we sometimes felt the sting of rejection from a few people at a time, but now we experience it in large, public venues. And worse than that pain is knowing that so many people witnessed that rejection . . . and are probably judging you for it.

But rejection for most of us began long before the first time we felt it online. Many of us experienced it early in our childhood. Perhaps, like me, it was during your elementary school years. Maybe it was in high school or college. Maybe it was in your family of origin. In any case, because of our personal experiences with rejection, we avoid certain situations at all costs. We have formed and fostered an unhealthy fear of rejection.

My fear of rejection has kept me from friendships, destroyed co-worker relationships, and later caused destruction in my marriage. It could have ended my marriage. It could have kept me from fulfilling my purpose, walking in my calling, and fulfilling the dreams God had given me.

If I had not learned how to overcome the fear of rejection, I would never have been able to write this book. I am so thankful for God's mercy and grace in this area of my life. It has taken me six years to write this book, and part of the reason stems from a fear of rejection.

Not the Vision I Thought

God planted the seed for this book years ago. In April 2011, I attended a writer's conference in Colorado with this book's proposal in my hand, and it was there that I began to see His plan to redeem this area of my life. Nearly every time I mentioned my idea to a conferee, it resulted in a ten-to-fifteen-minute conversation about how he or she struggled with the need for approval and how social media exacerbated the problem. I pitched it to agents and editors to mixed reviews, until I pitched it to one agent who wanted me to write it immediately. I was so excited, I could have screamed. Okay, maybe I did. A lot . . . by myself . . . in my room.

But here is where God's ways are so much higher than our own. On June 1, 2011, I was scheduled for surgery to have a carotid body tumor removed from my neck. My charge from the agent at the time was to go home, write my book, and start building my platform. I had two months to write a book and schedule speaking engagements. No biggie, right? Ha!

The subject of this book was important to me—I had realized I was an addict to approval, and I needed to work through and write through how to overcome that addiction. And that's when the fear of rejection became more apparent to me than ever before. What if I put myself out there and people rejected me? What if I wrote the book and nothing happened? What if no one reads it? The *what ifs* and the fear of rejection threatened to consume me.

And in the midst of all that, I had a tumor removed. That surgery was a defining moment for me, one that altered the course of my life forever. The removal of that tumor was the most challenging surgery and recovery I have ever experienced, but through it, God showed me how desperate my need for the approval of others was and how the fear of rejection was keeping me from fulfilling my calling.

About six months prior to my tumor removal, God placed a vision in my heart to unify the body of Christ in my community by transforming the lives of the poor through relational ministry. By the time I had recovered enough from the surgery to start pursuing work again, God had inflamed my passion to pursue the vision wholeheartedly. He made it overwhelmingly and abundantly clear that I was to go after the vision, regardless of what it cost me. In fact, not long after the surgery, I was let go from my job. I now had the time to work on that vision but . . . talk about feeling fearful and insecure! For the first time in my life, I was unemployed, temporarily disabled, and in a new town where I had few connections. I had two choices: I could let the fear consume me, or I could trust God and obey whatever it was He wanted me to do.

To pursue the vision, I had to overcome my fear of rejection and share the ministry idea with people I had never met before. Scheduling meetings with people I didn't know to share with them what God had laid on my heart took courage I wasn't sure I had. I could risk everything—my ego, my pride, my self-respect. And pursuing the vision also meant forsaking the idea of writing this book.

But I did it . . . even when the people I spoke to told me I was crazy. They told me my idea would *never* happen in this town, especially with me leading the cause. I was a nobody, a woman, an outsider. It wouldn't and couldn't be done by me. Some people liked the vision but couldn't see how we could bring the churches together to accomplish it. Some insisted there was no way to transform the lives of the poor, and others said we would never raise enough money because financial resources were already thin throughout the community. There were more people believing it couldn't be done than there were willing to believe that it could.

Despite the negativity, my willingness to overcome my fears and obey God increased, and He directed me to people who were encouraged by the vision. Then He pointed me to others who said they were willing to fund the vision. Volunteers appeared and organizational leaders began verbally supporting the cause. Answer by answer, God taught me how the fear of rejection would get me nowhere, but if I trusted and obeyed Him and His Word, I would see miracles happen. And I have.

How Bad Do You Want It?

Fear of rejection will keep us from the good gifts the Lord has for us. I believe it is the largest reason people don't experience their "promised land" or get to see their calling here on earth fulfilled. Fear of rejection is a destroyer of dreams; it can defeat any visionary. We must recognize the power this fear has over us and learn how to combat it.

But what if you don't believe you can overcome the fear of rejection? What if just the thought of trying paralyzes you? Then what? During my time of doubt, I began repeating this refrain to myself: "I'd rather be seen as a fool before man than stand before God and be deemed a fool before Him." It gave me courage.

If you want to succeed, you will have to draw some lines in the sand. Decide which is most important to you: will you allow the need for man's approval to rule you, or will you choose to obey God over all else? Allow me to suggest a few ways to help in the process of overcoming your fear of rejection and breaking your bondage to the addiction of approval.

First, you must decide that pleasing God is more important and urgent than pleasing people. John 12:42–43 says,

> Yet at the same time many even among the leaders believed in [Jesus]. But because of the Pharisees they would not openly acknowledge their faith for fear they would be put out of the synagogue; for they loved human praise more than praise from God.

It was too much for these influential people of Jesus's time to sacrifice the approval of others to follow Him. They chose human praise over God's favor and paid for it—eternally, perhaps. Jesus was standing right before them, clear as day, yet they were afraid to claim Him. If the fear of rejection was too challenging for them, how much more challenging is it likely to be for us, who must believe without seeing (John 20:29).

In my case, I had to realize that what God was calling me to was bigger than myself. I knew the plight of the poor. I'd heard their stories and had walked with them through difficult times. My heart had been broken over their challenging situations. The vision was bigger than me because I knew what was at stake. And though I sometimes felt alone in my quest, I was not.

God never calls us to do things that include only us. God's call on our lives will always include more people, more resources, and more talent than we could ever muster on our own. You may not even have clarity on what your call is just yet. I encourage you to seek God for it. His Word is true. Ephesians 2:10 says, "We are God's handiwork, created in Christ Jesus to do good works, which God prepared in advance for us to do." If the vision you feel Him calling you to makes the hair stand up on your arm and makes you shrink back in fear, that may be the fear of rejection. You will need to overcome it to reach the culmination of your vision.

Next, you must realize that trust is an intrinsic part of this process. Trusting God is vital to overcoming the fear of rejection. Proverbs 29:25 NASB says, "The fear of man brings a snare, but he who trusts in the LORD will be exalted." I get the sense that the author of this proverb wrote from experience. He knew it could be easier to follow man than God, yet his words encourage us to recognize that when we trust God, He will exalt us. If we allow ourselves to be trapped by the fear of others, we will lose the blessing God intends for us. There is blessing in trust and an exaltation that follows obedience. This should offer hope to all of us. There were naysayers in my journey and there will be naysayers in yours as well. But how strange is it that we so often choose to listen to those negative human voices when we could hear and follow what our gracious, loving God tells us to do?

Finally, you must obtain and maintain a razor-sharp focus. Jesus said that the enemy of our souls comes only to steal, kill, and destroy, but Jesus intends to give life in abundance (see John 10:10). If you give in to the fear of rejection, you hand the enemy the very weapon he will use to steal, kill, and destroy you and everything you hope for. If, however, you focus intently on seeking God, if you choose to trust Him and be obedient to Him whatever the cost, you will be blessed.

His Vision Is Better Than Ours

God gave me the vision for what has become The Link of Cullman County in 2010. In 2012, we received official incorporation papers from the state of Alabama. Since then God has allowed us to see over nine thousand lives transformed through this vision. In 2017, we were ministering out of twenty-six different locations, serving thirty communities, and had over six hundred generous donors supporting this vision. During the same time, our offices expanded from a single building to a campus of over twenty-two thousand square feet.

And I think to myself, "What if I hadn't obeyed? What if I had let the fear of rejection consume me? Where would the people whose lives have been transformed be today?"

It's time to decide what you will do with your fear of rejection. Will you allow it to rule you? Consume you? Will you choose, like the important people of Jesus's day, to seek the praise of others rather than the favor of God? Will you stay stuck in a snare of fear of other human beings, or will you trust God to exalt you when and how He chooses? Will you allow the enemy to steal, kill, and destroy all you hope to achieve someday, teetering instead on the edge of what could be, or will you choose the life of abundance to which God has called you?

How incredible would this world be if every one of us pledged to reject the fear of rejection, if we refused to let it keep us from doing the things God has called us to do! Imagine what could happen if the body of Christ became fools before men so that we might all stand one day before God and hear those beautiful words, "Well done, good and faithful servant" (Matthew 25:23).

In the following chapters, we will explore what to do next—how to put what we've learned into practice. It's time to decide how badly you want to walk in the freedom Jesus died to give you. Get out your highlighter, take out your notepad, and roll up your sleeves. This is where the hard work begins. You can't do this on your own, but your Father in heaven is more than capable of handling the heavy lifting. He just needs you to be willing to do the work with Him.

This is your turning point. It's time to choose. Are you ready? Let's do this.

Jesus, let us find our identity so deeply rooted in You that when people look at us, they see Your face. Help us not to allow the fear of rejection to consume us but to choose daily to trust You and obey You in everything we do. Bless our efforts so that one day, perhaps when we least expect it, we will look back and see not only our lives transformed but the lives of others as well, knowing that what You called us to do was bigger than us and our fears, and You were with us the whole way through. In Jesus's name, amen.

CHAPTER 9

One Day at a Time

• • • • • • • • • • •

Life is a matter of choices,
and every choice you make, makes you.

JOHN MAXWELL

Last week, I came home from work and found clutter everywhere. My seven-year-old had scattered toys by the door, all over the living room floor, in front of the television, into the breakfast nook, and on top of the table. Yet, as I looked around, I realized that the fault was not all his; I also saw shoes, bags, mail on the table and countertop, coats on chairs, and food and dishes piled up in the sink from breakfast—yesterday's breakfast.

No one was coming to feature my house on an HGTV show. I would not be taking pictures to put on Pinterest or Instagram or take the risk that one might someday pop up on Facebook's Timehop. My house gets like this occasionally, and when it does, I can become overwhelmed, almost paralyzed. I don't know where to begin to address all the problems I see in front of me, and I don't want to deal with it.

I have similar feelings at times when God shines a light on a new area of my life needing renovation. Anxiety, worry, concern, and, of course, shame rise within me and make me want to shut down rather than start working. I must remember in those situations that the state of my house—or my heart—is no surprise to God. Allowing myself to be overwhelmed by it all will lead me only deeper into discouragement; I need to ask God to help me take it one step at a time.

You may be feeling something similar at this point. You may be realizing that you have a lot to work on and you don't know if you are able to change it all. You may be wondering if it's possible to get out of what feels like a never-ending cycle of approval addiction. If so, let me say this: Breathe.

Take a deep breath in. Slowly exhale. If you need to, do it again. Doesn't that feel better?

I believe that together we can create a strategy for tackling each area we've discussed so far, so that you no longer feel overwhelmed but instead feel like you can focus on the areas where God is helping you grow.

Over the last eight chapters, we have explored a variety of emotions, outcomes, and challenges that all approval addicts face. Each chapter identified a struggle and offered some biblical direction for overcoming the problem. I hope you've learned something from these chapters, even if it was just a nugget of truth you can keep with you as you move forward on this journey. But let's face it, there's a lot of stuff in here. Just reading the chapters and praying the prayers at the end won't make long-lasting changes in our hearts, minds, and actions. That's a great start, but there must be more. So now what? Now we take what we have learned and put it into daily practice.

Your success or failure in the approval addiction cycle will depend on one thing: choices. Your daily choices matter. They will either aid you in overcoming your addiction or send you spiraling further into its effects. You can live out the rest of your days in recovery and freedom, or you can choose to stay in bondage. Staying where you are will further isolate you, delay you from forming healthy relationships, and strain your intimacy with God. Every day, moment by moment, you must choose how you will respond to your need for approval. To put it another way, you can choose to live in a home filled with clutter, or you can start picking up, one room at a time. Either way, you are making choices.

My friend Sherry says it this way: "It's the itty-bitty choices that either make or break an addict. Those itty-bitty choices will put an addict into relapse or help her walk in recovery." She's right. She knows exactly what it means to have your response to addiction determine your life or your death.

Sherry and I first met nearly four years ago in the Cullman County Detention Center. She was an inmate, and I was her Jobs for Life teacher. This was the second time I had the opportunity to teach Jobs for Life to women in the jail. Sherry was small but fierce. Shorter than me, she was blunt, loud, fast-talking, and gravelly voiced from years of smoking. She wanted to attend my class, but her name was not on the list. I am a sucker for someone with a desire to learn, so I made a place for her. I have no doubt that that decision changed everything—not just for Sherry, but for me.

We could not be more different. We both have baggage, but we come from vastly different family backgrounds. Sherry grew up dirt poor and experienced abuse throughout her life. She attended a school where no one cared if she returned the next day. I grew up in the middle class, in a loving family, and earned multiple college degrees. Sherry had life experiences I could not fathom. She'd had to fight for daily meals. Her father got her drunk at age seven and high at age eight. She dropped out of school before she finished the ninth grade. She'd been a prostitute, a drug dealer, a madam, and—in her own words—a thug. Her current stint in the detention center was her twenty-seventh—in *that jail*, not counting other sentences she had served elsewhere by the time she was forty-five years old.

This time, however, was different for Sherry. She was encountering God in a new and fresh way. Her ex-partner, who was also in the class—we'll call her Kathy—had urged her to seek God to find out for herself if He was real. That's when I and others from our ministry met Sherry. She'd never known that complete strangers could love her unconditionally. God began breaking down her walls, and in our classes, she learned a new way to live. When she was released, Sherry went to rehab, where she was able to put even more tools in her toolbox. At the time of this writing, Sherry is four years sober, owns her own home and car, is reconciled with family and friends, works several jobs, and is an encouragement to addicts, both those in recovery and those who still use. Every time Sherry shares one-on-one or with a group, she tells them, "It's your choices that matter. They will keep you alive, or they will be your death."

The truth of this statement touched us a bit too close to home recently. Sherry's ex-partner, Kathy, despite her early encouragement for Sherry to seek God, made different choices than Sherry. She had the same amount of support, perhaps more, than Sherry, but made all the wrong choices. A few months ago, Kathy made one last choice; she overdosed on heroin, killing herself. Her death is still a reminder to me of the difference between an addict who wants life transformation and goes after it fiercely and an addict who persists in making poor choices.

Your choices matter. You may not be pumping your veins with heroin to fuel your addiction, but ask yourself honestly how bad you felt the last time you experienced rejection. Now, you might be thinking, "Yeah, but this addiction could never kill me." I must disagree. Unfortunately, our community recently mourned the loss of a young mom who seemed to have everything going for her. She was happy, full of life, always giving of herself to others . . . at least on the outside. Inside, she was listening to lies, and she took her own life. Approval addiction may not produce track marks or open sores, but that doesn't mean there are not negative, destructive, suicidal thoughts on the inside.

This mentality is no different than that of a drug or alcohol addict. No one ever thinks they could get that low, that they would ever overdose—until they do. Even as approval addicts, our thoughts can be destructive, even deadly. Ask the mothers of children who committed suicide because their peers made fun of them online or at school.

An article written by Sam Laird on Mashable in 2012 states that from 1995 to 2002, as internet consumption grew dramatically, teen suicide skyrocketed. Suicide rates among girls ages fifteen to nineteen grew by 32 percent; among girls ages ten to fourteen, the rate grew by 76 percent. Many of these tragedies were connected to cyberbullying.[23]

The need for approval doesn't just affect us as addicts; it affects our children as well. Does our constant striving for approval model to them where their approval should come from? Does our frail sense of identity influence their self-image and self-esteem?

My son has a growing faith in Jesus Christ. But, like many others, he worries about what other people think of him. As a recovering addict, I know the signs and, because of my journey, I also realize how important it is for me to affirm my child for who he is in Christ. As often as possible, I talk to him about his identity and who God created him to be. So when he is worrying over what the kids think of him or how they have responded to him, I tell him, "Sawyer, God made you to be you. Worry about you. Let God take care of [insert name]." I have watched him grow from an insecure student at the beginning of the school year to someone who is more secure in his identity in Christ, because we work on it regularly. We pray about it on the way to school and talk about it when he is home. He feels comfortable in expressing his anxiety to me. I do my best not to criticize him for worrying about what others think, and I remind him that, most often, the only person he can control is himself. It's my hope that, by the time he gets to his teenage years—when knowing who he is, what he believes, and why he believes it matters even more—it will be so engrained in his head and heart that it will be natural for him to ignore the drama and just be himself.

Identity Determines Actions

If a woman knows who she is, what power does a bully—cyber or otherwise—have over her? If you understand that your identity comes from who God says you are, you can more easily navigate the dangers of social media or walk away from the bullying because your sense of identity is no longer threatened by what people are saying. With an identity firmly rooted in Christ, you know how to stand your ground or seek help when bullies threaten you. It's a process that will take time, maturity, and perseverance. It will not happen overnight, but it is important to take it seriously and start immediately.

As a side note, I want to remind you that bullying, harassment, and abuses are not only internal struggles we must face; they're also occasions to seek help. That may mean consulting a Christian counselor, speaking to a school principal or teacher, or filing a report with an employer or the police.

But on those occasions when God nudges you to realize that

you are seeking approval from the world and not from Him, I pose this question to you: "How badly do you want to no longer walk in bondage to other people's needs or expectations? How badly do you want to feel like you don't have to please everyone around you? If you want this, you will have to fight for it. You're already on the battlefield; are you ready? Put on the armor and prepare for combat."

You can expect to face major opposition as you start to make new choices. Remember, we talked about this in Chapter 3. Your opposition is not flesh and blood. It is not your spouse or your friends. It's not your mother-in-law or coworkers. It's also not the person who keeps trolling you on your Facebook page or other social media accounts. No. Your opposition is the devil himself, and he is out to keep you just as bound up as you have always been. Ephesians 6:12–17 says:

> Our struggle is not against flesh and blood, but against the rulers, against the authorities, against the powers of this dark world and against the spiritual forces of evil in the heavenly realms. Therefore put on the full armor of God, so that when the day of evil comes, you may be able to stand your ground, and after you have done everything, to stand. Stand firm then, with the belt of truth buckled around your waist, with the breastplate of righteousness in place, and with your feet fitted with the readiness that comes from the gospel of peace. In addition to all this, take up the shield of faith, with which you can extinguish all the flaming arrows of the evil one. Take the helmet of salvation and the sword of the Spirit, which is the Word of God.

Now that you are aware of the forces arrayed against you, perhaps you better understand that your enemy is not going to easily release you from an addiction to approval. I'm not telling you this as a scare tactic but as a reality check.

I'll be honest with you. I worry that something in this book has already spoken to you—you've realized you need to make a change, and sooner rather than later—but you've put that chapter and its teaching behind you and just kept going. You haven't sought God to make a change or, worse, you're still trying to do it in your own strength. I can tell you, weeks or months or a year from now, you're going to realize you're in a worse place than you were before—you're depressed, alone, struggling, and you won't know what went wrong.

That's why I want you to make the right choices now, while this information is still fresh in your mind, before bad habits and thought patterns creep back in. We must learn what the good choices are and how we can put them into practice. So grab your highlighter, pen, and notebook or journal (or, if you are reading this on your e-reader, get your highlighting tools and your Evernote link and do your thing). Let's make a plan to overcome.

You Need a Strategy

In Chapter 1, we talked about acknowledging our addictions. You took the need for approval test—remember? Since you are still reading this book, I will assume you failed . . . with flying colors. I mentioned then that some chapters would seem to be speaking directly into your situation, and other chapters might not feel pertinent to you at all. If that's true now, it's okay. It would be overwhelming to feel like you're struggling with every area mentioned throughout this book. People-pleasing, insecurity, control, personal offense, jealousy, anger, fear of rejection—those are a lot of issues! (Of course, if you *are* struggling in all those areas, be encouraged; I've been there, and I survived.)

Whatever your situation, we'll walk together through each area so you can have a few takeaways to start working on. I also suggest that you take a moment, right now, and ask God if one of those areas is more important or more urgent to deal with than others. Ask Him to reveal to you which of those areas is causing you the most internal struggle right now. Then rank each one in order, starting with one and ending with seven.

___ People-pleasing
___ Insecurity
___ Control
___ Personal Offense
___ Jealousy
___ Anger
___ Fear of Rejection

Now on the one ranked number one, write on the lines below why this area is such a struggle for you. You'll want to remember this for later when you are experiencing this behavior again.

_____

_____

_____

_____

_____

Now, create a goal for this area. For example, if you said, people-pleasing is your number-one ranked area, you could create a goal that says something like this, "I will use the Scriptures listed in the Appendix under people-pleasing and start memorizing one Scripture each week.

Write your goal here.

_____

_____

_____

_____

If you want to take this a step further, don't stop at just one goal. Get out your journal and go ahead and record several goals in each area. Keep in mind, we'll also dive in a bit more in the areas below on how to deal with each of these character traits. You may want to read through them all and then come back to this one again at the end.

Choose Your Mindset

In Chapter 2, we dug a little bit into what it meant to be a people-pleaser and how our brains are affected by the pleasure we receive from others' approval. The dopamine that is released at the moment of approval sends positive vibes throughout the body, leaving us wanting more of that "feel-good drug."

Remember how King Saul's need to please people led to his downfall. I want you to cling to these facts as if your very life depended on them: David and Saul were both good-looking, smart, and from unimportant families. Both were anointed to be king. From all appearances, they had equal opportunities. However, their outcomes were very different. Why? *Because David chose to please God, while Saul chose to please people over God.* (Highlight that sentence, underline it, put exclamation points next to it. It's vital.)

This is not complicated. We can have all the advantages and

"anointing" in the world, but if we choose to honor people and give them glory over God, we will be rejected by God and lose our chance at living out His calling on our lives. The choice we make here can land us in different roles, doing different jobs, and cause us to miss out on the special something wonderful that God had intended us to have.

Let Saul's story be the flashing neon sign that warns you: STOP! CAUTION! YIELD! Take a moment now and, on the lines below, write yourself a note reminding yourself who you want to be like—Saul, who chose to please man, or David, who became a man after God's own heart. Choose carefully. Your choices matter.

Breaking the Cycle

As someone who leads a nonprofit that constantly reviews how we can help people escape poverty, I understand that poverty is not limited to material things. Poverty has emotional, relational, spiritual, and mental roots and ramifications. We at The Link of Cullman County constantly seek God to show us new ways to help others break the cycle of poverty that they have been living in for so long. It is difficult, however, because many people don't even realize that they are caught in a cycle. So it is with the cycle of approval addiction. We repeat the same behaviors, not realizing there might be an alternative route, another way to respond.

In Chapter 3, we dove into the issue of insecurity, which is the root of the approval issue. If we are uncertain or insecure about who we are, we will end up acting like someone else. We will allow other people to define our character traits, talents, and identity. We learned from the example of Eve how we can see ourselves as God's image bearers, that we can know who we are and respond to any situation according that identity.

So how does an image bearer live? Defeated? Frustrated? Feeling like a failure? Of course not. If we are His image bearers, we should reflect the image of our Creator. When we consider who God is, would any of that be consistent with His character? No. But how can we know that for sure?

It's time to pull out your Bible or open your Bible app and search for Scripture verses that describe who God is and, in turn, who you are because of Him. And yes, I said *verses*. That's plural. Start by searching your Bible for seven verses to read, repeat, and remember until they seep into your inmost being. The Bible says, "Love the Lord your God with all your heart and with all your soul and with all your strength and with all your mind" (Luke 10:27). The best way to love God with all your mind is to learn His Word. Embed it in your mind so there is no room for those old ways of thinking.

Now, using the cycle that we discussed in Chapter 3, we'll take the seven Scripture verses you've found and write them in each area of the cycle. Or you can use the worksheet in the appendix of this book to keep for later. Record each Scripture, so that when the next attack comes—and it will—you will be better equipped to recall who you are and who you were created to become. Learn to recognize a spiritual attack for what it is, so you can tell the devil, "God really did say I am . . ."

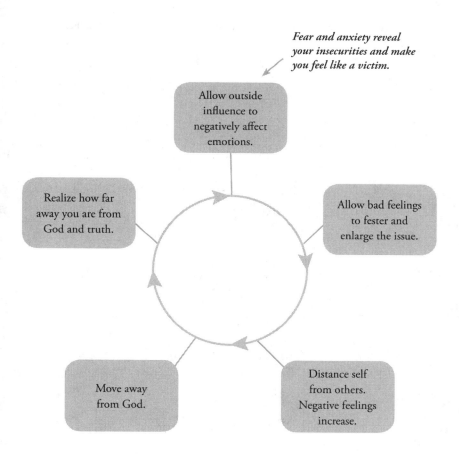

Fear and anxiety reveal your insecurities and make you feel like a victim.

Allow outside influence to negatively affect emotions.

Allow bad feelings to fester and enlarge the issue.

Realize how far away you are from God and truth.

Distance self from others. Negative feelings increase.

Move away from God.

Allow outside influence to negatively affect emotions. (Main emotions: fear/anxiety)

Allow bad feelings to fester and enlarge the issue. (Main emotions: guilt/shame)

Distance self from others. Negative feelings increase. (Main emotions: Bitterness, anger, resentment)

Move away from God. (Main emotions: unworthiness, lacking peace)

Realize how far away you are from God and truth. (Main emotions: lost, loneliness due to separation from God, unforgiveness, discouragement, depression)

If you are having a hard time finding seven, do not worry. We will go through a few more of those in a page or two. There is also a list of Scriptures in the appendix of this book. Just keep in mind that those Scriptures helped me and have become a part of my recovery. However, yours may differ. God can and will use Scriptures that you find in your life. My list is there if you need it, but make this more an opportunity to explore God's words for you than to duplicate what is listed in that section.

If you write the Scripture you find into this book, take a moment later to copy it on a sheet of paper that you can carry with you. This way, when we're finished, you can take that list and tape it to something you see every day, such as your bathroom mirror or in your Bible. You can also use the blank chart that can be found on page 183 Start praying those Scriptures over yourself every day as protection. You will not always immediately recognize an attack—our enemy is tricky and always scheming (2 Corinthians 2:11)—but being aware can help you better avoid being caught in the cycle again.

When you catch yourself feeling ashamed, guilty, or depressed, you can return to your list, wherever you've chosen to place it, to remind yourself how to pray until the enemy flees from you (James 4:7). I promise, if you make this a habit, the attacks will become less frequent. As you learn how to use Scripture to speak against this vicious cycle, you will start to understand how it feels to walk without the shackles of addiction wrapped around your mind and heart.

You're a Control Freak

So, you're a control freak. Join the club. Many others are right there with you. I am a self-confessed control freak, but I am learning to let it go, like Elsa in *Frozen*. (That girl knew what she was talking about . . . all that releasing and singing and letting her hair down. Come on, ladies, you know you wish you were her. Surely I'm not alone here?)

Control freaks tend to drive people away; no one wants to live up to someone else's crazy expectations (I know, I know. Your expectations aren't crazy; mine weren't either. *Wink, wink*). As approval addicts in recovery, however, we must recognize that God created people to do the things He has called them to do, the way He has called them to do them. Sometimes His way looks quite different from the way *we* think it should be done. But just as God made you, He made the people around you too. He knitted each of them together in their mothers' wombs (Psalm 139:13). He gave each a purpose and a calling only they can fulfill. If I truly believe those things, then putting all my expectations on other people short-circuits the unique ideas, plans, stories, experiences, and perspectives God has planned them.

In Chapter 4, I shared how God taught me the hard way about His plans versus my plans. I learned that He is a God who gives and takes away and that I needed to learn to surrender both gains and losses to Him. So now, I'm asking you to make a list of every person who is not meeting your expectations. Even if it takes up all the pages in your journal, write down their names. When you are finished, ask God to help you surrender each of those people back to Him. They are already His, of course. But when you try to control them, it's like playing tug-of-war with the God of the universe. And here's a little secret: He wins. Every time.

Some people and some disappointments may be easier to release than others. Some names you may need to write on a piece of paper, hold them in your hand, and then crumple, tear, and physically release them (into the trash bin, for example). But freedom will follow surrender. Every time.

Don't Choose to Be Offended

Five simple but powerful words: Don't choose to be offended. In Chapter 5, we learned that we have the power and authority through the Holy Spirit to choose not to be offended when someone disappoints or hurts us. When others don't do what you think they should have done—even though you offered your thoughts on the matter—don't choose to be offended. When someone unloads his anger on you and you can't figure out why, don't choose to be offended. When the woman in line behind you makes a comment about something you're wearing, don't choose to be offended. When your husband does not compliment you on the new shirt, dress, shoes, nails, or hairstyle, don't choose to be offended. When your boss fails to recognize your hard work, don't choose to be offended.

Instead, choose forgiveness. Choose grace. Choose love. These are your new choices. You know who you are, and you know that whatever is said (or not said) has nothing of value to speak to you. Your identity is not dependent upon their approval, acceptance, or praise. You live to please God. Period.

Compared to What?

Community, not comparison, is how we show the world that our Savior is alive and lives within us. Jealousy, envy, and strife reflect poorly on us, the Church, and our Savior. In Chapter 6, I encouraged you to take to heart Paul's words to the church in Ephesus: to "walk in a manner worthy of the calling to which you have been called, with all humility and gentleness, with patience, bearing with one another in love, eager to maintain the unity of the Spirit in the bond of peace" (Ephesians 4:1–3 ESV). Be someone who uplifts, encourages, bears with others, and seeks unity.

Let's put that in action. Right now, ask the Lord to reveal to you one person or entity that raises envy within you. Once you've called them to mind, thank God for them. Thank Him for their existence, their birth, or their foundation. Thank God that He created them uniquely in a way no one else could duplicate. Acknowledge that you are sometimes jealous of them. Then thank God for the ways He created *you* to be unique, for how He's set *you* apart for His purpose.

Think about it. Comparison is just another word for coveting. Exodus 20:17 says, "You shall not covet your neighbor's house. You shall not covet your neighbor's wife, or his male or female servant, his ox or donkey, or anything that belongs to your neighbor." Recognizing this, our next step is to repent. Clearing our hearts of coveting helps us to see our neighbor with God's eyes, rather than our own.

Finally, pray blessings over them. Pray that no weapon or attack would prosper against them (see Isaiah 54:17), but that instead God would bless them financially, emotionally, relationally, and physically. Ask God to heal their innermost wounds or illnesses. Ask Him to bless their families and their businesses so they would increase in number according to His will.

How did that feel? Do you still feel jealous, or has your perspective changed? It is impossible to pray for someone for very long and maintain a spirit of jealousy. Every time I have done this, I soon feel like I can walk alongside the other person and celebrate their successes, encourage them in their calling, and support them in their goals—and I can do so not being the least bit concerned about what God will do for me. I have more humility, gentleness, and love for them, and I am more eager to seek unity with them and be joined to them with bonds of peace.

Our natural tendency is to compare ourselves to others, but when we take our eyes off the people and things around us and pursue community instead, our perspective changes. That is how we can experience the oneness Paul mentions in Ephesians 4:6. Oneness is what we are shooting for—today, tomorrow, and forever.

Do You Have a Good Reason to Be Angry?

In Chapter 7, we studied what God said to Jonah when the people of Nineveh repented. As Jonah complained, God simply asked, "Do you have a good reason to be angry?"

When we consider all we have learned so far—what Christ has done on our behalf, knowing our sins, our failures, and our weaknesses—what do we have to be angry about? At times in my life, I have been a little like Nineveh. What a wicked mess I was making of my life. And yet God showed that He is gracious, compassionate, slow to anger, abundant in lovingkindness, and more than willing to relent from sending calamity (Jonah 4:2).

We have no control over what others may do or say, but we always have a choice about how we react. We can choose to be angry or we can choose to be like our Father—gracious, compassionate, slow to anger, kind, and forbearing. Do we want to be remembered for our anger or self-pity, or would we prefer to be remembered as image bearers who reflected our likeness to the Father's graciousness, compassion, and kindness? Is there even a question? Surely not.

On the approval addiction cycle that you have been working on, write these words next to the third box: "Do you have a good reason to be angry?" Above it, write out Jonah 4:2, so you can see how you need to respond instead of in anger. Be prepared. I promise: This verse will enter your head as you're spouting off to someone in anger. It will also pop up in the middle of your own private pity party in your head. The Holy Spirit will remind you of it when you least expect it. When that happens, be grateful. God is reminding you how to be more like Him. Don't do what Jonah did. Repent and choose life. In doing so, you'll learn how to live free from the addiction of approval.

Don't Fear Rejection

In Chapter 8, we discussed the fear of rejection and what happens when we live in bondage to it. We looked back at our need-for-approval cycle to see how we are so easily caught in this trap that puts us in a place of vulnerability. No one likes to be vulnerable. But I encourage you to press in; don't back away from it. Ask God why you feel so vulnerable. Is there a wound you need Him to heal? Do you need to forgive someone who hurt you so you can move forward? Find out what it is that makes you feel so vulnerable. Much of my fear arose out of past failures and my tendency to assume each time would be just like the others. I relived negative experiences repeatedly in my head. It was a hurdle I had never quite gotten over. And then the barrage of "what ifs." What if this happens? Or what if that *doesn't* happen? "What ifs" can make you crazy. We must decide, we must choose to overcome those fears. If we don't, they will paralyze us. We discussed how we can overcome our fear by deciding that praise from God is more valuable than the praise of other human beings.

You may also recall that I urged a razor-sharp vision on you. We must learn to tune out the world and all its noise. Let me suggest here that you get your hands on some good goal-setting materials. I like to use Lara Casey's Powersheets,[24] but if you want a different approach, a quick Google search will help you find tools that suit you. Take some time alone with the Lord and ask Him to give you vision, focus, and even a Scripture verse or two to define your task and motivate you. Turn off your devices or social media notifications and grab some books that get you excited about your area of passion. Give yourself some time to do this. Think about marking off a week or two or even thirty days to reset and refocus.

God's good plans for you seldom spring up overnight. You will usually find them one step at a time—one faithful, obedient, trusting step at a time. You won't always get it right, either. Some days the fear will win, but you'll know God's mercies are made new every morning (Lamentations 3:22–23). Get up the next day and remember to trust God. Then obey what He tells you, and make a fresh start.

A New You

There it is—everything we've covered in the last eight chapters, broken down so you can start using what you learned today. You have enough now to start making immediate changes, by choosing new thinking patterns, making Scripture part of your daily routine, and prioritizing freedom as more important than what others think of you.

But there is more to learn in this journey of recovery. That's why this isn't the end of the book. Over the next few chapters, we'll study what we can expect as we grow in these areas, make new choices, and break the cycle. Isaiah 43:19 encourages: "See, I am doing a new thing! Now it springs up; do you not perceive it? I am making a way in the wilderness and streams in the wasteland." This is the good stuff. This is what you get if you follow through on what I suggest and let God lead you through it. Don't give up on us yet. We've got a few more chapters to go.

Jesus, I love You so much. Thank You that You are the Word who became flesh. You chose to come to earth as a babe to live among humanity so that I could learn from You how to be a true image bearer of God. Teach me more about You and reveal those areas of my life that are not congruent with Your Word. Teach me more about my identity in You. Renew my mind with Your Word. Show me how to experience supernatural peace and joy. Help me to surrender every day of my life to You. Amen.

Know Who You Are

. . . .

But you . . . are a chosen people.
You are royal priests, a holy nation,
God's very own possession.

1 PETER 2:9 NLT

Y ou are a failure." Those words had taken up space in my head
for way too long. I had learned they weren't true, but they kept
creeping back into my thoughts like a spider and its web. I would
sweep away the web one day, but it would reappear the next. I'd
try to ignore it, but slowly and surreptitiously, it spread again until
it covered all my thoughts. The lies had taken over, and they were
determining both my thoughts and my actions.

It all started because I'd been shown a number. I look at this
number every week as the director of The Link of Cullman County.
It helps us as a ministry to determine the state of our funding and

whether we can pay our bills. It's far from my favorite part of the job, but it is one of those other job duties I've been assigned. The number was negative that week—significantly so. In fact, it was a how-in-the-world-are-we-going-to-keep-our-doors-open negative number, the kind that sent me into panic mode. My mind exploded with questions—How did we get here? What are we going to do? How are we supposed to raise that much money in four days? How will we make payroll? Can I afford to not take a paycheck this week? What should I do?!

Then came the firing squad of worry, fret, and anxiety. The shots ricocheted off the walls of my mind. In desperation, I shifted into action mode. "I won't find any answers just sitting here," I told myself. "Get up and do something. Make some calls, maybe write some emails. Who can I ask for that sum of money?"

A week went by as I tried (and mostly failed) to focus on the work at hand. Staff members came in asking for things they needed to purchase. Every request induced more panic. Time seemed to speed up as payday approached; even the mail-in donations seemed as dry as Death Valley.

The more I flailed to find a solution, the more those words clamored in my brain: "You are a failure." I was praying for a miracle, but the big check from an anonymous donor never came. What I did receive, however, was a lesson from God.

Thursday came, and my sweet friend and colleague, Milli, came in to ask how I wanted to handle the bills. It took everything in me to share my battle with her. There still wasn't enough money in our account. Tears streamed down my face. I felt shame and guilt over my inability to make the dollars appear.

"I feel like a failure," I told her. "I feel like I'm letting everyone down. I'm tired, and I don't know how I can keep going like this. I appreciate now why so many nonprofits and their leaders shut down—they're burnt out within five years. This is hard work. I don't know if I'm strong enough to keep going."

Milli fastened her gaze on me. "You are not a failure. You can't believe that. You know this is just a rough patch; it's like this every year."

"Yes, I know. But I'm tired of it. When does it get better? When do we get to sit back and take a breath and not have to worry from month to month?"

She didn't have any profound answers; she just encouraged me to keep moving forward. Later that day I got this email from her:

Subject: Hey

Hey—I just wanted to tell you that you are not a failure! Jesus says you are blessed and highly favored! He doesn't make no failures.

It broke me. It still breaks me every time I read it. She was right. I knew she was right, but sometimes it feels good to know that someone else realizes it too. It gave me a whole new outlook on our situation. It also reminded me that I was getting way too caught up in what everyone was going to think of me instead of listening to the truth of what Jesus says about me.

Stop Beating Yourself Up

All that week, I had been beating myself up. Milli's email reminded me that sometimes we need to just put down the stick. You know, the invisible stick we pick up to torture ourselves with while we brag about what failures we are. It's the mindset that refuses to believe we can define who we are. That tells us we'll never change. The one that loves to throw around all those hurtful, negative words that make us feel less than what we are.

With Milli's help, I finally remembered to reach for the sword of truth. I remembered who I truly am and that my identity is not wrapped up in a number. I'm not defined by how much money I'm capable of raising from month to month. I'm not the sum of my capacity to make and keep relationships with donors, staff, or volunteers. My value is not found in the sum of my book sales or determined by whether this book stays here on my computer for my lifetime or is published and placed in bookstores around the globe.

The number of "likes" I get on a Facebook post does not determine my identity. Neither is it wrapped up in how many subscribers I have on my blog or whether people watch my YouTube video. The number of hearts I receive on Instagram or how many friends or followers I have in any of those social media platforms does not, cannot, and will not determine who I am. My identity has nothing at all to do with how I do or do not perform.

My identity is defined by God alone. I am who He says I am. He is my Creator, my Maker, the Author of my faith, and the Lover of my soul. He is the One who sets me apart and deems me worthy, even when I feel incapable of doing anything that seems fruitful for the day. My identity is who God says I am, not what a bank balance or some other measurement says. I am reminded that God "doesn't make no failures."

How about you? Are you under pressure because of what you think other people expect from you? Do you feel constantly burdened to perform a certain way for your clients, family, or employer? Does the incessant need to succeed rattle you a bit? Do the lies swarm like locusts in your mind, whispering into your subconscious all the ways you are failing today?

You do not have to live this way. You can choose to believe differently; you can live life from a place of security, where your circumstances and thoughts do not determine your beliefs and actions. You do not have to accept society's view of your successes or failures. No. Instead, you can rest in knowing and owning who your Creator says you are.

You Are Not Your Own

You're not good enough. You messed up again. You are such a failure. You looked so foolish. You're never going to get it right. Nobody thinks you can do this, you should just resign. He gave you this ministry, and you're running it into the ground. You're useless; you never do anything right. Surely, there is someone else who can do this better than you.

Words like these ran on a continuous loop in my head. But God knew I was ready for change. Milli and her email broke loose inside me a reminder that I was God's. I belonged to Him. In fact, He'd made me who I was, the way I was, on purpose! Sure, I'd messed a few things up. My plans were proving to be less than perfect. But His plans are always perfect, and I am part of them. If I could let go of my plans and my ways and my . . . everything, He could make me new again. It wasn't up to me to make the ministry work. It wasn't up to me to make my family work. It wasn't up to me to be perfect.

It was up to Him. I—and everything about me—belong to the One who bought me back from sin.

You and I, prior to our decision to submit our lives to Christ, were separated from Him. There was nothing we could do to earn our way into relationship with Him. We could not pay enough money, we could not be good enough, we could not pull ourselves out of our empty way of life. There was nothing that physically, emotionally, and most importantly, spiritually made us His.

Until Jesus made the way. Jesus came as a once-and-for-all sacrifice for the sins of the world. Through His sacrificial death, you "were bought at a price" (1 Corinthians 6:20) and "redeemed from the empty way of life handed down to you from your ancestors"

(1 Peter 1:18). Jesus paid the price, the unpayable penalty for our sins. He took our debt of sin, paid it off at the cross, and said to every human being, "It is finished."

When humanity was separated from God, we did not lose the image of God, but our sin blinded us to that core of our identity. We believed that our identities were wrapped up in failure—we were naturally mess-ups, misfits, liars, gossips, adulterers, and drunkards. We were unkind, angry, bitter, jealous, greedy, selfish, and so on. Because we believed those lies, we thought our identity was whatever we or anyone else decided we were. But when we choose to recognize those thoughts and actions as sin, when we repent and make Jesus Lord of our life, when we accept His death as the penalty for our sins—everything changes.

Everything.

When we surrender, we are no longer our own. All we are and have becomes His. We take up our rights and lay them down at the cross—including our full identity. Remember 1 Corinthians 6:20— we were bought with a price.

Don't run by that like a Black Friday shopper.

You. Were. Bought. With. A. Price. You might have been that one item left on the clearance shelf, the one no one wanted. But God sought you out, picked you up, looked you in the eyes, and said, "This one is Mine."

Physically, emotionally, and spiritually, you are His now. Everything about you, including your identity.

He Decides Our Identity

Understanding that our identity comes from God is the root issue we must wrap our heads around. We are not who our enemy says we are. We are not who the world says. We are not who our angry family member accuses us of being. We are not numbers. We are not defined by our performance or lack thereof. Neither, in our true identities, are we addicts. Revelation 12:11 says that it's "by the blood of the Lamb" that we have overcome our enemy. We who believe have taken up the identity that our Father—our Purchaser, our Owner—has given us. Second Corinthians 5:17 says, "Therefore, if anyone is in Christ, the new creation has come: The old has gone, the new is here!"

But maybe I need to stop for a moment and ask: Have you accepted Jesus's sacrifice on the cross as payment for your sins?

I can name the date and location where it happened for me. I remember how separated I felt from God the day I made the decision, and I recall the freedom I experienced afterward. I was twenty-six years old, and it was June 23, 2011. From that day forward, everything changed. But that is my experience.

Maybe you've been following Jesus since you were a child. Maybe you've taken a slow, circuitous route to come to Jesus, and you're just now drawing near. Whatever has gotten you to this point, I invite you to take a moment and ask the Lord, "Do I truly know You?" And be willing to hear His answer.

If you grew up in church, it's possible you've always felt like a part of the family without ever saying a definite yes to Jesus. Or maybe you've been drawing closer to Jesus for some time but you still haven't crossed the line and fully surrendered your life to Him. You know who you are; I don't. But I can't go further here without urging you to be sure that you will never stand before His throne and hear Him say, "I never knew you" (Matthew 7:23). Don't let anyone else define your relationship with Christ but Him and you. It makes the hair on my arms stand up to think that there will be churchgoers who hear those words as they seek entrance to heaven. So again, I ask you to examine your heart.

Some of you will come to the conclusion that you do not truly know Him. Not in the way we've been talking about here, as your

Owner, your Savior, your Lord. Or maybe you'll realize that you really have strayed from Him. It wasn't until now that you understood how far you've gone. If that's the case, I ask you to pray to receive forgiveness for your sins, recognizing that the power of this is not in the prayer itself, but in what Jesus did for you on the cross. Pray with me; use these words to start your conversation with your Lord.

Jesus, I am sorry. I realize that I have been acting the part but have not truly repented of my sins. Forgive me for all I have done and for all that I will ever do. From this day forward, I make You Lord of my life. I choose to follow You and Your commands, to trust You and obey You in all that I do. You paid the price for my sins when You died for me on Calvary. It was a price that only You could pay . . . and You did that for me. Today I give You my whole self, and as I do, I know that the old is gone and the new has come. Help me to walk in the newness of life You have purchased for me. Teach me all about the identity You have given me and not the one the world has tried to place on me.

If you prayed that prayer, then you are a new creation today. And I, along with every angel in heaven, am cheering with you at the proclamation of your newly professed faith in Jesus. Take just a moment and put today's date right here: _____. If you have a Bible, write this date in it as a reminder; if you don't have a Bible, then get one as soon as possible. This is a day you want to celebrate and remember forever. For me, remembering this date each year reminds me of my commitment to my Savior. Consider doing something special in remembrance of it, something that will bring glory to God. My son gave His life to Christ when he was six years old. I want him to always remember the day he made that decision. So, on that day, we celebrate his new life with a trip to the frozen yogurt store, and I read to him his salvation story, which I wrote in his Bible after his commitment date and baptism.

I also urge you to be baptized. Don't wait. There is something supernatural that God does in the process of baptism, providing a physical representation of what happened spiritually in our heart, mind, and spirit. Consult a local pastor to learn more about baptism. Every church is different, but I encourage you to seek out baptism as the outward expression of what has happened in your heart.

Now What?

It all comes down to this: *You are who God says you are, because you are His.*

No one can change that, redefine it, or make it into something else. That means now you can fully accept the things He says about you in His Word—that you are blessed and highly favored, holy, part of a royal priesthood and a holy nation, a delight to Him, a child of God, an heir to the throne, seated with Him in heavenly places, and the apple of His eye.

If you didn't know such things are said in Scripture about you, I suggest that you open your Bible or browser and search each of those terms. Make sure you read the actual verses first; blogs and commentaries are helpful, but it is best to hear the words your Father has to say about you before you hear what anyone else says because— remember!—your identity comes from Him, not from the ideas or opinions of others.

Can you imagine how differently we might respond to people around us if we, as the body of Christ, truly understood this? How would each of our relationships look if we no longer sought to be affirmed by people because we already knew that our God—the One who gave Himself to purchase us—affirms us? Would the challenges we face throughout the day be easier to confront and conquer because we'd know who our Father is? Would we be better parents—free to discipline with love, provide firm boundaries, and speak encouragement to our children, regardless of their attitude and actions—because we're no longer trying to please them or keep them happy?

Are you seeing how the knowledge of this truth could change our world, our lives, our futures, and generations to come? We have a choice; we do. We can realize that we have been bought with a price and glorify God through our bodies by responding by faith in Him and in our true, God-given identities—or we can continue to live in bondage to our own ideas and others' impressions.

I think it's time to clean out the cobwebs that have accumulated in our minds. We are not failures. We are not mistakes. We are not the sum of our weaknesses. We are children of the King. Heirs to His throne. Blessed and highly favored. That's our identity. Let's choose to live our lives in faithfulness to who we are and whose we are and not to the lies we have believed.

Father God, You are a gracious God who has shown Your love to us since the beginning of time. Your Word gives us multiple physical examples of how You are our Creator and Owner. Everything, absolutely everything, we have is Yours, including our identities. God, today we ask You to help us start believing all the sweet words of truth You have said about us throughout the Bible. You do not make failures, mess-ups, misfits, or mistakes. We are fearfully and wonderfully made and unconditionally loved by You. Thank You that who we once were is now gone and the new is come, through the price Your Son, Jesus, paid on the cross. We are Yours. May we walk in the full understanding of this today, in Jesus's name, amen.

CHAPTER

11

Obsession
(Not the Perfume)

· · · · · · · · · · ·

Everybody has an obsession; mine just happens to be you.

CURIANO.COM

I'd like to introduce you to my friend Jill. She is also a declared approval addict and is learning daily how to walk in recovery. It might be why I initially liked her so much; she gets me and I get her. Jill is driven, intelligent, organized, and a loyal friend. We met while I was working at Miami University. I was the Interfraternity Council (IFC) Advisor, more specifically the advisor to thirty-one fraternities and to the IFC executive board. Jill was a student. Our paths crossed initially because she was a member of Kappa Delta sorority and the vice president of communications on the Panhellenic executive board. I was the advisor assigned to check in once a month with her. Jill is one of those people whom you just like when you first meet her. She is pretty, outgoing, and simply a nice person. She is also nearly six feet tall—so she has that going for her as well.

Our relationship blossomed when she stopped by my office in August of 2001. It was the summer after I'd made a commitment to follow Jesus with everything in me, and she spotted one of the *Left Behind* books sitting on my desk. It prompted her to ask if I was reading that book and whether or not I was enjoying it. As a new believer, I had thrown myself into getting to know this Jesus guy by reading my Bible, Christian books, and journaling. This meant I read whenever I had a chance, including lunch breaks. Even though the book was out in the open, I was caught a bit off guard by her mentioning it. Once I got over my initial shock, I realized it might be an opportunity to share.

After chatting a bit about the book and her interest in it, which was mutual, we learned that we had both committed our lives to Jesus that summer. She, however, had yet to grasp how to read the Bible and wondered how I had learned so much about it, basically on my own. I invited her to attend a Bible study. After a few times in study together, she asked if I would be willing to disciple her. I really had no idea what that entailed, since I was so new to the spiritual thing myself.

I was being discipled by a young woman, and she and my Bible study leader encouraged me to start meeting with Jill one-on-one to share what I was learning. I realized pretty quickly that discipling means doing life together. When questions came up, if I didn't already know the answer, we dug into the Word of God to find them. It wasn't long before I discovered that I loved discipling women (something I still enjoy today).

It was in one of our meetings that Jill presented me with her dilemma. She was getting married that summer and had been offered a job in Chicago, to start right after the honeymoon. Her fiancé was supportive of her and would go anywhere she wanted to go. But she was challenged by the idea of moving away from their family and friends. They highly valued these relationships, and the prospect had unleashed a lot of fear about uprooting her whole life.

The conversations about her moving began dominating our meetings. She was starting to obsess over it. Should she go? Was it worth the aggravation and upheaval of her whole life? Would they be able to find new friends? Could they find a church to attend? Would it hurt their new marriage? Although the pay was good, was it enough to live in Chicago comfortably?

She shared how she had talked to everyone she knew about this dilemma, but people's responses were split. She just could not figure out what God wanted her to do, and she desperately wanted to do the right thing. And that, in her mind, meant making a decision that would ensure everyone's happiness.

Each week as we met, this question would make its way into our conversation. So one day, we were at Jimmy John's for lunch, and her frustration leaked out of her mouth. "I wish God would just give me an answer on a neon sign," she said. "It would make this decision so much easier!"

I think most of us are like Jill. When a decision like this comes our way, we want to do what is best for everyone. We want God to approve, our friends to declare their excitement for us, and our family to be proud. It would make it so much easier if God would just put our answers on neon signs so it would be overwhelmingly, abundantly clear what we are to do.

But it doesn't usually work that way, so we start obsessing over it—tossing it around in our minds day and night, seeking our friends' and family's opinions, logically considering every angle. Sometimes we say we'll pray about it, and we do. But then that turns into a tug-of-war with God, and the dialogue eventually leaks out of our mouths.

LIKE ME OR NOT

Jill's statement sits in my memory as if she'd said it yesterday. It leaked out right there in the Jimmy John's sandwich shop with all the amazing bread smells wafting from the oven, mixing in with the aroma of lunch meat and all the fixings—it makes my mouth water just thinking about it. The irony is that Jimmy John's is filled with signs. Signs that make you laugh. Signs that make you reflect. And signs that make you wonder if you should have spent time reading that sign at all. That might be why that analogy came to mind for Jill that day.

After a moment, I said to Jill, "If you could take a guess, what do you think God is saying? What if He's already given you a sign? What if that sign is to trust Him, to walk in faith with Him, and not try to figure everything out? What if He is asking you to be willing to go wherever He takes you, believing that He has your best interest at heart?"

She stopped for a moment, then said, "I never thought about that before. If God put the answer on a neon sign, it wouldn't require much faith at all."

Can you relate to this situation? You have two good options, but you can't make up your mind which way to go. Maybe you're trying to choose between jobs or finding a new career. Perhaps you are perplexed with whether you should stay home with your children or obtain employment. Or you're debating on moving or staying. You are tossing and turning your dilemma to figure out what you are going to do. Your mom thinks this; your spouse says that; your best friend has another idea. Maybe you've even posted your dilemma on Facebook, looking for advice. You want so much to make the right decision, the best decision, but you're paralyzed, wishing you could see what lies ahead, and finding yourself obsessing over which choice to make.

Selfish or Sacrificial

I get it. It's not always easy to choose which route to take. Particularly as an approval addict who struggles with needing to know everyone's views before she can make a decision, big or little. This has been my challenge for most of my life. There have been times when I, like Jill, have chosen to obsess over other people's ideas about what I should do. I know I should seek direction from the One who possesses all the answers, but my need for approval from those around me obscures my path.

Here's the truth: Our God in heaven has a clear view of what is ahead and already knows which direction you need to take. No obsessing needed. He can help you discern what to do, regardless of your situation. Even when you feel stuck at the fork in the road, you can lay out your fear to Him and trust His plan.

It's taken me years to understand this concept and experience the fruit of it in my life. It all boils down to two verses of Scripture, found in Romans 12:1–2.

> I urge you, brothers and sisters, in view of God's mercy, to offer your bodies as a living sacrifice, holy and pleasing to God—this is your true and proper worship. Do not conform to the pattern of this world, but be transformed by the renewing of your mind. Then you will be able to test and approve what God's will is—his good, pleasing and perfect will.

At first glance, those verses may seem like a strange combination. One talks about offering your body as a living sacrifice in worship to God; the other encourages you not to conform to this world but be transformed by the renewing of your mind so that you can "test and approve" God's will. Huh? What does one have to do with the other?

Those verses are often taught separately from each other, as if giving ourselves to God is distinctive from being transformed by renewing our minds. They can feel like the two roads—two separate ways to go and two different decisions to make. But God used these two verses to bring new clarity and understanding to my need for approval.

The key to sacrificial living—to honoring God by sacrificing our fleshly desires, inclinations, and plans—is in the mind. That is where it all begins. The only way we can learn to offer our bodies as a living sacrifice is to teach our minds not to conform to this world. When we renew our minds with the Word of God, we will know which choice aligns with God's Word and which does not.

But it doesn't stop there. These words of wisdom help us understand the importance of living sacrificially versus living selfishly. Sacrificial living helps us turn our thoughts and focus upward. Selfish living keeps us focused on the opinions of others.

How do we renew our minds? Study the Bible. Pray according to the Word so that our *wants* align with God's desires. We take time to fast from things that encourage us to conform to this world—social media, television, movies, etc. This may even mean we take a break from talking to people about our decisions. Although a bit challenging, I can tell you from experience that it's a journey that leads to freedom.

Put into practice the principles you learn so they become actions and not just beliefs. For example, take a true Sabbath—a day of rest in which you do no work, but rest, relax, and read books that are life giving and gospel based. Meditate on a single Scripture verse throughout the week, asking God to reveal the fullness of the verse. Walk in nature and look for Him there. Spend time with a friend or family member who you know spends time in the Word. Ask him or her to share their study or prayer techniques. We are all at different places in our spiritual journeys, so I encourage you not to see this as a list of obligations, but rather as practical suggestions for renewing your mind.

Consuming electronic media often impedes the renewing of your mind. The images and sounds to which we expose ourselves are often designed to convey a message or promote an agenda that does not align with the Word of God. The light of God's Word will restore your soul, but the light of a screen will sap your spiritual energy. The entertainment industry is too often a distraction from the greatest adventure of your life—following Jesus and learning to obey God's will.

Renewing your mind—focusing on God, His Word, and what it says to do—will transform your life into a sacrifice that pleases God. Staring at your phone will not. Binge-watching Netflix will not. And a funny GIF on Facebook won't do it either.

Test and Approve God's Will

Jill's desire of wanting to have a definitive decision plastered on a neon sign is not so far-fetched, from what we find in the Word of God. In fact, Romans 12:2 says we can claim access to the knowledge of God's will for every decision we make. It states, and I believe this promise, that if we choose to renew our minds, "then [we] will be able to test and approve what God's will is—his good, pleasing and perfect will." That is clear enough to me. Renew your mind in His Word, and you will know if your decisions are approved by God— good, pleasing, and perfect.

Notice that these verses don't say anything about whether your mother will approve or if your roommate will think it's a great idea or that your social media followers will still support you. They do, however, remind you to examine your prayers to be sure God's will is at the center of them.

When our minds are focused on—or better yet, obsessed with—seeking God's will rather than the approval of people, we will experience the pleasure and blessing of achieving His good, perfect, and pleasing will.

A Different Kind of Obsession

As approval addicts, obsessing over what other people think can consume us. Trying to base our decisions on what pleases everyone else is impossible. Learning to wait on God for our answers will crucify our addicted flesh and teach us how to gain wisdom. James 1:5 says, "If any of you lacks wisdom, you should ask God, who *gives generously* to all without finding fault, and *it will* be given to you" (emphasis added). We will not get to experience the generosity of God if we don't wait for His timing to deliver it.

It is only by learning that our lives are meant to be lived in a sacrificial offering to God, not to meet our own needs, that we will experience freedom from this addiction.

What a Difference It Makes

Jill and I have been friends since 2001. We live in different states now, but I recently had the chance to visit with Jill and her family for eleven days—and even that length of stay did not feel long enough. During my visit, Jill was preparing for a women's conference for which she served as director, and I got to witness her renewed mind in action.

Though Jill and I are similar in age spiritually, I am five years her elder. She has been like a little sister to me, and watching her lead a conference that hosted over 450 women, displaying faith deeply rooted in God, made me extremely proud of who she has become.

She organized, planned, and executed the event, utilizing a support team, encouraging them to believe God for the impossible, and seeking Him every step of the way. I saw a woman committed to prayer throughout her week, clinging to God when issues popped up, and, as would be expected, motivating her team to do the same.

She has spent years learning and growing in God's Word, and though she would tell you she still struggles with wanting the approval of others, in my opinion, Jill today is much more rooted in who she is in Christ than she could ever have imagined when we first met over a decade ago. Jill is an excellent example of what it looks like to live as a sacrificial offering to God, not conforming to this world but renewing her mind to be transformed by the Word of God.

Your Transformation

What would it look like if we took hold of these verses in Romans 12:1–2 and chose to live them sacrificially, not seeking to satisfy our approval needs? What would it look like in *your* home as you respond to your spouse? Would it be easier to submit to your husband if you knew God's wisdom was given just as generously to him as it is to you? Would you slow down your decision-making process to allow your husband time to also seek God's direction and answers? Would you work through the decision together, instead of running ahead—or over—your husband to please everyone else?

What about your children? Would you react differently if you were rooted more in God than in worrying whether or not they like you as a mom? Imagine how different things would be.

You see, when we lay down our need for approval and allow God's Word to guide our choices, we begin to experience freedom from the bondage of other people's expectations. Living this way frees us from worrying what others will think; it takes off the chains of approval, roots our security in God, and allows us to make decisions following God's good, perfect, and pleasing will. And then, we no longer need to obsess; instead, we can rest in knowing He already approves of us.

Here are a few suggestions you might consider if you are struggling to know if you are obsessing or if you are waiting on answers from God:

1. **Have I prayed about this situation?**

   If you have answered yes to this question, good for you! You may need to be patient with God for His answers. If you answered no, you should pray now and proceed to question number two.

2. **How long have I been contemplating this decision?**

   If your answer to this is countless hours, days, or even weeks, it may be time to admit you are obsessing. Perhaps you could try using 2 Corinthians 10:5 as a reminder to yourself to take every thought captive and make it obedient to Christ.

3. **If you are still unsure of what to do, have you searched the Scriptures for an answer?**

   The Bible has a wellspring of wisdom; ask God to direct you in what to read to help guide your decision. This is not a suggestion to open your Bible and hope it lands right on that exact Scripture you need. Pray and be patient with this process. His timing is not ours. If He does not lead you at first, pray again and again. There may be some other character traits He needs to work on in you before He reveals His answer. Take the opportunity to learn and grow. You cannot learn patience until you have to actually be patient.

4. **How many people have you spoken with, and have they guided you back to God's Word for answers?**

The Bible tells us to go to others for godly advice. Proverbs 19:20 says, "Listen to advice and accept discipline, and at the end you will be counted among the wise." Proverbs 12:15 (NASB) says, "The way of a fool is right in his own eyes, but a wise man is he who listens to counsel." People can be helpful with navigating tricky situations. However, if they are not pointing you to the ultimate Provider of wisdom, I would suggest they are not helping but rather delaying. The best godly friends I have encourage me to seek my answers through God and His Word, and then pray with me as I come to my decisions. They do offer their own opinions, but always with the caveat of testing what they recommend against the Word of God.

These are just a few questions you can ask yourself as you seek God in the next decision you need to make. By focusing your thoughts on His perfect will, instead of obsessing over everyone else's approval, you can find freedom.

Decide today to be a person who chooses God's will over your own. Seek Him deliberately for wisdom to avoid self-absorbed decisions that will only please those around you. Present yourself as a living sacrifice that brings glory and honor to Him.

Father God, You are good, You are perfect, and everything You do is pleasing. Make me into a woman who offers up her body as a living sacrifice to You every day. Guide me in the decisions I have to make, so that my life gives honor and glory to You. Help me not to conform to this world, but rather, by renewing my mind with Your Word, help me to live a life of obedience to You. Help me test and approve every situation that comes my way, knowing that You will guide me to that which is good, perfect, and pleasing to You. In Jesus's name, amen.

Peace Junkie

• • • • • • • • • • •

When the power of love overcomes the love
of power, the world will know peace.

JIMI HENDRIX

The 1960s was a turbulent period. The decade was marked by turmoil and conflict from policy divisions, racial clashes, and generational strife unseen in many generations."[25] "[It] changed American life and culture more profoundly than any other ten-year period in the twentieth century."[26] Civil rights demonstrations, peace marches, Vietnam . . . stymied by challenges at home and abroad, the US could not seem to find peace, no matter how much people craved it.

By the end of the 1960s, the hippie movement culminated in Woodstock, a gathering in upstate New York from August 15–17, 1969, that brought together people of all ages, races, and demographics for "peace, love, and rock 'n' roll." There had never been anything like it in American history. There was plenty of rock 'n' roll, but drugs and sex were more in evidence than peace and love.

What many people discovered—and what is still true today—is that those things are only temporal. The drug fix and the sexual fling offer fleeting pleasure, at best. They never truly or lastingly fill the longing for peace we all have within.

I wasn't even a thought in my mother's mind in the 1960s; I would not come into being until the next decade. But I wish I could have told those folks what I know now about peace—that even in the middle of conflict, when your world seems to be spinning and you feel like you are losing control, you can find peace.

Is it true? Can we really come to a place of inner calm in the midst of conflict? Even when everything around us is going crazy? I think so. I believe it because of what I and others have experienced despite the chaos around us. But the only way to achieve that peace is to pursue it.

Pursuit of Peace

I am a full-time wife, full-time mom, and full-time ministry executive. That's a lot of "full-time" going on. There are many people who count on me, who want me to live up to their expectations. They want me to do things the way they expect me to do them, and often they expect me to anticipate their needs when they haven't figured out themselves what those needs are.

It isn't difficult for me to fall into the trap of trying to please all those people, but doing so leads me to grasp for control as I manipulate things—and sometimes people—to get my way. When I let it happen, I am left feeling caught in complete chaos, unable to find anything even close to resembling peace.

Perhaps you know how that feels. In fact, you may know far better than me. But what if we changed? What if you and I no longer worried about what our kids or husbands were up to? What if we didn't care about how much money was in our bank accounts? What if we weren't concerned about that promotion at work or the next raise we could earn? What if we could wake up without worrying about the entire next week? Better yet, what if we could go to bed at night without worrying what the next day will bring?

What if you didn't have to be concerned over what your spouse or boyfriend was doing—whether He loves God as much as you do or is just going through the motions? What if you didn't need to worry about how you will afford the repairs you need to make to your car, your house, or your stove?

Well, it can happen. I'm not saying our problems will disappear. But I think we'd be surprised if we decided with our whole hearts—starting now—that we were going to pursue peace with everything we have in us. Psalm 34:14 says, "Turn from evil and do good; seek peace and pursue it." My favorite version of this verse comes from the Amplified Bible, where it says, "Depart from evil and do good; seek, inquire for, and crave peace and pursue (go after) it!" (AMPC).

What if we did that? What if we became so passionate about peace that we stopped at nothing to experience it in our lives? What if we craved it? I crave a lot of things—chocolate, a bowl of ice cream . . . But what if I started to truly, deeply, and passionately crave peace?

Better yet, what if you and I became known for our peace? What if others started asking questions about how we always seem to be at peace? Then what? And what if how we live from this day forward changed radically because we decided—right here, right now—to seek, no, to *pursue* peace?

Would you be willing to do that? To at least consider it? Because I want to share with you how we can be seekers of peace. In fact, I want to show you that if you believe in Jesus as your Lord and Savior, you worship a God who *is* peace. And that is why we must be seekers of peace. We must pursue peace with such fervor that we crave it like a meal after a long fast.

It was only a few years ago that I realized the importance of seeking peace. Without it, life is chaotic, crazy, and out of control. But with it, I am calm, wise, patient, and willing to allow God to do what He wants to do. I no longer feel the need to rush into what I want to do. Instead, I experience joy and more of what Jesus talks about in John 10:10, where He says He came to give us abundant life.

I want peace. I must have peace. I am continuously pursuing peace.

A Virus, a Gallbladder, and a Tumor

The first six months of 2011 were difficult and chaotic for me. My life was full of conflict, challenges, and tension. It seemed I could not catch a break or find the peace I was craving.

I started the new year with a virus that the doctors thought was mononucleosis, then later decided was not. A definitive diagnosis was never made. At first, the virus left me mostly tired and rundown, then it turned into a stomach virus, and that revealed gallstones. A month after that discovery, I had to have them removed.

While in recovery, I visited an ear, nose, and throat (ENT) specialist to have a lump on my neck checked. I had lived with the lump for years. It never caused any problems and was inconvenient only when I had a throat-related illness. But with my recent trip to urgent care for the mysterious virus, I decided it might be time to get it looked at by a specialist. I'm so glad I did.

A CT scan revealed I had a "carotid body tumor." The carotid body is the area or mass right at the base of the carotid arteries. Those arteries feed blood to the brain and heart. My tumor, though benign, needed to be removed. In the decision-making that followed, God led my husband and me from one doctor to another until we landed in the hands of one of the best ENT surgical teams for carotid body tumors in the United States. This kind of tumor is rare, and it was important that I be with a doctor who knew what he was doing. Had we chosen the first ENT specialist we consulted, mine would have been his first surgery of this kind, and I probably would not be here to write this book. The surgeon we eventually chose, however, had twenty-plus years of experience, and although the tumor is rare, he had over a thousand surgeries for this specific kind of tumor under his belt. We discovered that was more than any other surgeon in his field. His experience with my rare tumor turned out to be a very good thing.

The initial CT scan did not tell the whole story. To the human eye, the tumor seemed to be relatively small and in a location the doctor thought could be removed with only a small grafting of my artery. What only God knew, however, was that the tumor had veins growing through it. Those veins made the tumor grow faster than anticipated and made it act like a living organ. What was expected to be a routine two-and-half-hour surgery turned into six and a half hours. The team removed a six-inch vein from my leg to replace the artery that was removed from my neck. I needed four units of blood during the surgery. And what should have been a simple recovery is still in process years later.

One or two things are likely to happen when you walk through a health-related crisis like this. Chances are, you will either seek advice from every person you meet (and they will give it to you), or you will quickly learn how to hear from God. If you follow the first, you'll end up questioning every little move you make. But if you grasp the second, you will experience the peace that passes all understanding. In that place, no one's advice or disapproval matters; following God's lead is what counts.

Guard Your Heart with Peace

God taught me some incredible lessons during this time that still guide me today. I can't help but think about the person I once was—a needy, controlling, untrusting woman who tried to fill her daily cup with every bit of encouragement and praise she could grab from the people around her. (I'm not saying that I don't still struggle with this; of course, I do. I am still in recovery. But those times are less frequent now, and where I once had to know what everyone thought before I could make major decisions, now I know I can trust God for the good things I need in my life and not worry about what He is doing anywhere else.)

How did I get to that point? I learned to surrender control to God and feel the peace mentioned in Philippians 4:6–7, which says,

> Do not be anxious about anything, but in every situation, by prayer and petition, with thanksgiving, present your requests to God. And the peace of God, which transcends all understanding, will guard your hearts and your minds in Christ Jesus.

The need for approval is just another word for worry, anxiety, or stress. Let's try starting the verse this way: "*Do not desire other people's approval about anything.*" Seeking someone else's approval to resolve our inner conflict is like a dog trying to lick peanut butter off of his tongue. It may keep us busy (and it may be hilarious to others), but it's going to keep us focused on ourselves. It takes the focus off God and puts us in the center of our world. The people in our lives will feel obligated to fulfill our every need—but they never will because we are constantly thirsting and hungering for more. Addicts always want more.

These verses became a promise to me. They helped me see how

God offers me peace when I surrender my anxieties, worries, and cares to Him. That's when He can do His job as Ruler of the universe. When I get out of the way, I let Him be who He is as the focal point of my world.

If you are willing to take your addiction, your need for approval with all its worry and anxieties, and leave the whole smelly mess in God's hands, then He will do something marvelous with it. He will take it from you and give you His peace in exchange.

The more we choose to willingly obey God, to seek Him in prayer and petition, to thank Him for who He is, the more He, the God of the peace that passes understanding, will guard our hearts in Christ Jesus. And that is exactly what we need to overcome our addiction: a guarded heart, one that is not seeking everyone else's approval but is instead full of sweet, calming, all-consuming peace.

As Elsa sings in *Frozen*, let it go—all that stress and worry about what other people have thought, are thinking, or will think about you. It's gone. You have peace. Crave it. Seek it. Pursue it.

Lord God, we want to be seekers of peace. Please make Psalm 34:4 real to us. Deliver us from our fears; help us seek the good things and not the evil that we crave. Help us pursue Your peace with new passion and desire. We want to cast all the worry, anxiety, and fear we have of what others think of us at the foot of the cross and leave it there, never to pick it up again. Psalm 103:12 says You will remove our sin from us "as far as the east is from the west." No one else can do that. Father, we turn from our sin and seek You. Please guard our hearts in Christ Jesus through Your everlasting peace. Let us seek Your peace. Help us release every person around us from any expectation that they should produce peace in us. Only You can supply the true and lasting peace we need. Thank You. In Jesus's name, amen.

A Joy-a-Holic

• • • • • • • • • • •

Joy does not simply happen to us.
We have to choose joy and keep choosing it every day.

HENRI J. M. NOUWEN

D id you ever wonder if the guy who wrote the book of James (you know, James) lost his mind? I have. I mean, really. Who would "consider it pure joy . . . [to] face trials of many kinds" (James 1:2)? Not me, that's for sure. Trials are not a joy. They are hard and frustrating. They make me feel uncomfortable and stretched in ways I don't like. They are inconveniences. In fact, until I studied that verse of Scripture and understood it, I thought it was ill placed. I thought it must have been a mistake. Choosing joy and facing trials? Those concepts felt like they were not just unrelated, but opposites. How in the world could anyone think that the first could lead to the second? James must have lost his mind, and the men who decided to place this book in the Bible must have ignored or missed those verses and focused on the section below them that talks about seeking wisdom from God. Obtaining wisdom from God at least makes sense, but not this joy-in-trials stuff.

You think I'm kidding? Check it out yourself; it's plain as day in James 1:2–4. It says:

> Consider it pure joy, my brothers and sisters, whenever you face trials of many kinds, because you know that the testing of your faith produces perseverance. Let perseverance finish its work so that you may be mature and complete, not lacking anything.

I avoided this text for years because it felt so foreign to me. Then one day, the words seemed to leap off the page and smack me upside the head to help me see a bit more clearly.

My husband and I were struggling to know what we were supposed to do with our lives. We had recently uprooted our lives—out of what felt like obedience to God—to move from Ohio to my husband's hometown of Cullman, Alabama. We were soon baffled, confused, and a little upset with God over our circumstances. The local church we had been so sure would take off like wildfire barely sparked. All the dreaming we had done, all the plans we thought were totally orchestrated by the Lord, had fallen flat and shattered like crystal on a cement floor. Even thinking back to those days feels hard, still today.

My husband was in his hometown, so the fact that the church did not succeed as we had expected was particularly hurtful for him, because it felt like a personal failure. We decided to seek God in prayer and fasting, asking Him to reveal to us why in the world He'd moved us from our comfortable home in Ohio, a home we'd loved, to Cullman, a place that had rejected our attempts to make it better.

The Lord began to speak to my heart in a variety of ways. He taught me about the importance of my choices and how they can build my character during times of trial and struggle. And then I stumbled upon the book of James as I was searching for Scriptures about seeking wisdom from God. Have you ever had that happen before? You're seeking an answer from God concerning one part of your life, and He responds by addressing an issue in a whole different area? Goodness, I hope I am not alone in that.

Anyway, there it was: James 1:2–4. The concept was so odd to me that I decided to look into the guy who wrote this book, James. I learned he was possibly Jesus's brother, and he had written the book to Jews who were new followers of Jesus. Wait. Weren't most of the books of the New Testament written to the Jews? No. Paul was passionate about taking the gospel message to the Gentiles, and his letters were to largely non-Jewish churches. But James had a heart for winning Jews for Jesus. In fact, James has been called the most Jewish book of the Bible.[27]

I haven't mentioned it so far, but I grew up in a Jewish family. Both of my parents are of Jewish descent. So, for that reason, the book of James quickly became special to me. James was not writing to a nebulous group of people; he was speaking to "my" people. Better yet, I felt as if he were speaking to me.

That personal connection led me to do some digging to understand what James was saying about joy amid trials. So I got a commentary, and the Lord used that commentator's words to deepen my understanding and show me that I had a choice in times of trial and struggle. I could decide to be grumpy, or I could choose joy and allow God to work on my character. The commentary also referenced Romans 5:3, in which Paul tells followers of Jesus to "glory in our sufferings" because, just as James suggested, doing so will build character.

Well, I didn't particularly want to hear about building character. I was struggling. God had chosen to make our lives inconvenient and uncomfortable, and all He wanted to talk about was character! Look at all we'd been through already. We'd moved nearly 450 miles from home. Our house in Ohio still hadn't sold. We had not-so-great renters living there and a grumpy property manager. Our toddler had landed in the hospital with pneumonia, our dog was attacked and nearly killed in my in-laws' yard, my husband couldn't find full-time work, and we were barely making ends meet. To top it off, I was a Yankee living in the Deep South, where I knew no one.

And God wanted to talk to me about things like perseverance, hope, and lacking nothing at all? I wanted to tell God what I thought about all this. After all, enough is enough. Hadn't we endured enough?

Apparently, God had another message for me because, as I studied and complained, it became apparent that I wasn't struggling with inconvenience or even the lack of comfort. The house not selling wasn't our trial. Neither was it me living far away from home. It wasn't my husband's dream not coming to fruition or his being unemployed. No, what I was struggling with was shame. I feared what other people thought about our perceived failures. Our church launched and collapsed in a matter of four months. People—friends and family—had financially supported us, prayed for us, and helped spread the word . . . and to what end? What made it worse was that another church had launched about a month after we did. They had more money, more people, and more resources. They were from out of town, not natives like my husband, yet they thrived and grew, while we struggled and shrank. It didn't matter; all I could see was, we had failed.

The epiphany hit me like a ton of bricks. Our trial was not because of all we had been through; it was because of how much we cared about what other people thought. That changed everything.

Suddenly I understood why James was telling me to "consider it pure joy" when I faced trials, because now I had a choice: I could wallow in shame and pity or choose joy and learn to persevere and build character. It taught me something significant about my circumstances, and I hope it can teach you something about yours.

You can choose to get caught up in what others think of you, adding unneeded drama to your circumstances. Or you can choose not to. You can choose to change your attitude during your struggle. You can decide that your value and worth are not in job titles. You can refuse to define yourself by success or failure, and thus avoid becoming sad, irritated, and self-absorbed. James's words speak life to the approval addict because they remind us to choose joy in our trials and stop seeking the approval of everyone around us. When we do that, we'll discover that in God we lack nothing, including His approval.

What does it look like to seek joy in our trials? I think it looks like my friend Peggy. Peggy and I are close in age. We both have blond hair, and we are both transplants to Cullman. We both have been married and divorced, and we both have children. Beyond that, Peggy and I have lived vastly different lives. In high school, Peggy ran away from an alcoholic father. Hoping for a fresh start, she landed in Cullman with some family members. She dropped out and married her high school sweetheart. She got pregnant with her son, and then a year later with her daughter. Things got hard, and her husband started using drugs. With the drug use came abuse. To cover up the shame and guilt, Peggy too started drinking. The alcohol numbed the pain within and helped dull the pain of the bruises on the outside as well. Before she knew it, Peggy's life had spiraled out of control. Protective Services removed her children from her home and placed them with other family members. Her marriage fell apart. Fearing for her life after her husband nearly beat her to death, she moved out. She was homeless the first time I met her.

Peggy came with a few others to The Link Center in the hope of getting a hotel room. She told me a sad story about how she and her friends needed to get out of the elements; they were ready to get clean and just needed a place to stay. Pulling on some financial resources we had, I booked her and her friends in a hotel room. She told me later that they got drunk in the hotel room that night, and before long she was back on the street. When Peggy and I met again, it was in the Cullman County Detention Center. She had signed up for the new Jobs for Life class I was offering to female inmates.

She seemed familiar, but I didn't immediately remember meeting her before. I learned in the first class that was she was tired of being tired and was ready for change, but didn't know how to go about it. She had recently rededicated her life to Christ, and I could see the potential for change. I wanted her to succeed. I admired how much she smiled despite having no teeth. In fact, her smile and laugh were so contagious that, if Peggy started laughing, the rest of the class would soon be in fits of laughter.

Like many of the women we minister to in the jail, Peggy realized that I could be useful to her as a way out of jail. It might sound like a bad thing, but it was part of the reason we were there; we believed that if we could begin a relationship with the women on the inside, we could help them become successful on the outside. Sometimes that works; sometimes it doesn't. With Peggy, it worked to her benefit in the long run. In the short run, however, the court's patience had run out, and she was sentenced to a stint in state prison. In Alabama, that meant Julia Tutwiler Prison for Women. In 2013, Tutwiler was recognized as one of the ten worst prisons in the United States. I worried that the Peggy I knew would never return.

I was right, but not in the way I expected. God used Peggy's time in Tutwiler to refine her. She took more classes while she was there. She called and wrote me often, telling me how God was changing her heart, mind, and life for the better. He was setting her free and healing her of childhood wounds. At the end of her nine months in prison, I picked her up to take her to her next destination, rehab. I didn't know what condition she would be in when I signed her out that day or what to expect on our two-hour drive back to Cullman. But Peggy taught me the truth of James 1:2.

She shared how she had learned that she had choices—choices that could help to keep her sober, develop healthier relationships, and make positive choices in attitude. She had learned to stop worrying about what other people thought of her. She said she had to make herself, her relationship with God, and her sobriety her top priorities.

Peggy showed me that joy in the midst of trials looks like a forty-year-old blonde with a beautiful, toothless smile. And I was not the only one to see that. I visited Peggy in rehab, and every woman living there told me how contagious her joy was. Even when they were tired and didn't want to work, Peggy always found a way to make them laugh. She has chronic pain in her back, arms, and hands and, as a recovering addict, can't take pain medication—but Peggy continues to post online, praising God, trusting Him for healing, and believing that He has a plan for her life.

Peggy's trials are still numerous, but God has honored her obedience to His Word by teaching her perseverance and how it feels to lack nothing. On the day I wrote this chapter, I congratulated Peggy on Facebook for her fourth anniversary of being clean. She attends church, she has a home of her own, and her two grown children are back in relationship with her, which means she enjoys her grandchildren too. She has a job cleaning homes.

Addiction can be hard, whether it's addiction to approval, food, substances, or something else. But there's always a choice. We can choose to consider it pure joy when we walk through our challenges, or we can choose the opposite: sadness, bitterness, and depression. I think one of the beautiful things about James 1:2 is not only the admonition to experience joy, but also the reminder that God gives us the freedom to choose it. He doesn't force it on us. He doesn't make it imperative; instead He invites us into relationship with Him, allowing us to choose a better response to our trials.

What a different place our world would be if we understood the power of our choices. I'm so glad James figured it out and wrote about it. When I get to heaven someday, I hope to meet James, the brother of Jesus. I'd like to tell him how my opinion of him and his words changed over time. He isn't a lunatic at all. In fact, he might be one of the wisest men of all time. He figured out the secret we all need to know, especially those of us who are seeking victory over addiction: *Joy is the key to overcoming our need for approval.* Not joy for the sake of joy, but the supernatural joy that is the product of choosing God's will instead of our own.

Want to be a joy-a-holic, instead of an approval addict? Choose the joy God offers, and in doing so, you'll gain perseverance, which will produce character, and with character, you'll lack nothing.

Father, we praise You for Your Word and the fruit that it produces in our lives. As women who seek healing from our addiction to the approval of others, we want to see ourselves as You see us. We no longer want the dim and dreary pictures we paint of ourselves. Help us to choose joy even in our trials—especially in our trials. In times of waiting for Your answers and in struggles with our flesh, remind us how You are maturing us. Help us be complete and perfect, lacking nothing. Change us with the truth of Your Word, and let us consider it pure joy when we face trials of all kinds. In Jesus's name, amen.

The Surrender Habit

● ● ● ● ● ● ● ● ● ● ●

Surrender is not a battle of the will;
it is an act of worship.
WORKINGWOMANOFFAITH.COM

We are nearing the end of this study, but before we get there, there is an important principle in recovery that we must address. People all over the world have found and received healing in their drug and alcohol recovery because they work a program called the Twelve Steps. Bill Wilson and Dr. Robert Holbrook Smith, known to Alcoholics Anonymous (AA) members as "Bill W." and "Dr. Bob," founded the first twelve-step fellowship in Akron, Ohio, in 1935.[28] They created the program to help individuals overcome addiction, compulsion, and other behavioral problems.[29] In the first few steps of the program, participants come to the realization that they are powerless over themselves and their behaviors, and they submit themselves to "a higher power." We know, of course, that the higher power is the one true God, so we won't debate that point. But through the principle of surrendering ourselves to something bigger and more powerful than us, recovery can begin.

Fifty-five years after the twelve-step program began, a pastor from Saddleback Church in Lake Forest, California, created a version of the twelve-step program that addresses "hurts, habits, and hang-ups" from a biblical perspective. The program is called Celebrate Recovery.[30] This program gives churches a way to minister to those who are hurting and wounded. The principles are universal and can help anyone dealing with anxiety, codependency, compulsive behaviors, sex addiction, financial dysfunction, drug and alcohol addictions, eating disorders,[31] and more. Celebrate Recovery not only addresses the presenting problems people have, but also identifies the often invisible root causes of the problem. Like AA, Celebrate Recovery begins with recognizing that the person is powerless and needs God's help.

The common denominator of these programs is surrender. Typing those nine letters on the page is easy; the action is not. But surrender is not only imperative to your healing, it is also something you will come to crave as you see the blessings that come from letting go. In fact, surrender is not only the path to freedom, but also the armor that protects you from the enemy's attacks.

To receive healing, we must live our lives in the daily recognition and awareness that God is in control and we are not. This requires deliberate action. Every time we are confronted with the need to seek approval, to compare ourselves with someone else, or to feel angry over missed expectations, we will remind ourselves to submit our minds and hearts to the Lord. This must become a daily, even moment-by-moment, habit of clinging to our Savior in complete submission.

Surrender is a choice made every day. I know this is true because I had to surrender again just the other day. I was at a writer's conference, where I was looking for an agent to represent me and an editor interested in publishing this book. After my first day of pitching the idea, several people had expressed interest. It only takes one yes to get the job done, but I was proud of my collection of approvals for the day. Obviously, these experiences can be a huge test for the approval addict, like an alcoholic walking past a bar.

Later that evening, I went to grab dinner and caught up with a sweet new friend who was also having a good day. She listened to my news, then shared hers with me. It was so fun to celebrate our wins together. But as I listened to how well her conversations had gone with some of the same people I had spoken with, thoughts of comparison crept in, and I felt my joy gradually slipping away.

That negative voice in my head taunted me. "They liked her more. Her book will be better than yours." I know that voice too well; it works hard to convince me to give up; it loves to size me up against other people and declare me the loser. I could easily allow myself to get swept away in this dialogue—I've done it before. Unless I'm careful, I could soon be avoiding my friend and letting the enemy win. I'd be missing out on any potential gift her friendship might have held for me. But, I remind myself, I can declare that voice null and void because I do not need the same approval my friend received.

Even as a recovering addict, you will never be completely immune to the desire for approval from others. God has designed us all with a need for approval, but He allows us to choose whether we seek it from Him or from man. Over time, choosing Him does get easier, especially if you learn from Scripture and develop new habits to help deal head-on with issues when they arise.

This meeting with my new author friend was far from my first challenge as an approval addict, so I knew that I needed to immediately surrender my thoughts to God. I knew I was not going to win the battle on my own. So I repented and surrendered to Him. His Word tells me that I am to love my neighbor as myself. On this occasion, that meant letting go of my jealousy and rejoicing with her; after all, that's how I would have wanted to be treated. I wanted to rejoice with her, not just while we were together, but also later, when I was alone with my thoughts.

Then I remembered that the antidote to jealousy is prayer. I prayed for my friend—for her ministry, that God would show her favor at the conference, that her book would gain a contract, and that her story would be told to transform lives around the globe. I prayed for her family, and I asked for protection against the attacks of the enemy.

I wish I could tell you that my whole perspective changed immediately. It didn't. It doesn't. Sometimes I need to pray for hours, possibly days, because the temptation to compare and be jealous will still be there. I prayed continuously about this through the rest of that week. But God, in His kindness, prepared my heart for what she needed.

Later in the week, one of our speakers gave a powerful message about how God will use our weaknesses for His glory. The immensity of that message still brings tears to my eyes as I write these final words about my own weakness. When the speaker concluded, my friend came over to tell him how she was impacted by his message. I was standing nearby as well, and since he was speaking to someone, she and I connected while she waited.

I suddenly sensed God saying, "Pray for her." So I wrapped her in my arms and prayed. I don't even remember the words I shared, but I know in that moment God used me to speak a prophetic word over her to keep going, to write her book, not to give up, and to let her weakness become her greatest strength in Him. She thanked me for praying for her and then repeated her gratitude for the prayer almost every time I saw her until the end of the conference.

I assure you, those words came only because God had already been working on my heart to be in community and not in competition with her. He'd already taught me to surrender to Him, to know that His plan is greater than my own. Knowing that helped me to remember that what He has in store for my sweet friend is greater than what she thinks or can even imagine. There is no need to compare because He loves us both.

You must come to a place of full surrender for healing to happen in your life. If you have not already, I encourage you now to get down on your knees and tell God that you cannot do this on your own. Go ahead—you can admit you don't even want to try.

You can use words like those in the first step of Celebrate Recovery: "I admit I am powerless over my addictions and compulsive behaviors, my life has become unmanageable. I know that nothing good lives in me, that is, in my sinful nature." Romans 7:18 finishes out that statement: "I have the desire to do what is good, but I cannot carry it out." These words could not be more perfect for us as addicts. Is that not how we feel most every day? We desire to do good, but actually following through—well, that's a whole other story. Our natural, human response is still to seek the approval of others in every situation, and we'll only conquer this addiction if we surrender daily to the Holy Spirit.

Defining *Surrender*

The word *surrender* means different things to different people. I asked some of my friends on Facebook to tell me what the word means to them. Their answers included: to give up; to release control; to let go of my own plans, dreams, and thoughts; to trust without being in control; relief; and—one of my favorites—open hands.

If you consult the dictionary, you'd find a definition like this: "to yield to the power, control, or possession of another upon compulsion or demand; to give (oneself) up completely or agree to forgo especially in favor of another; to give (oneself) up into the power of another especially as a prisoner, to give (oneself) over to something (such as an influence)."[32]

As is so often the case, Jesus provides the ultimate example of surrender. As betrayal, arrest, and crucifixion approached, He faced multiple moments of surrender. In the upper room with His disciples, He told His betrayer, "What you are about to do, do quickly" (John 13:27). He wrestled with the Father in the garden of Gethsemane, but finally prayed, "May your will be done" (Matthew 26:42). While enduring the agony of the cross, He cried out, "*'Eli, Eli, lema sabachthani?'* (which means 'My God, my God, why have you forsaken me?')" (Matthew 27:46). It's likely He was reciting Psalm 22, which He certainly knew by heart. Though it isn't recorded in the Gospels, Jesus might even have continued thinking or praying the psalm, which inserts repeated words of surrender amid expressions of agony and rejection:

You are enthroned as the Holy One; you are the one Israel praises. In you our ancestors put their trust; they trusted and you delivered them. . . .

I am poured out like water, and all my bones are out of joint. My heart has turned to wax; it has melted within me. My mouth is dried up like a potsherd, and my tongue sticks to the roof of my mouth; you lay me in the dust of death.

But you, Lord, do not be far from me. You are my strength;
come quickly to help me. . . .

They will proclaim his righteousness, declaring to a people
yet unborn: He has done it![33]

It is even possible that Jesus's famous last words—"It is finished" (John 19:30)—might have coincided with the final words of
the psalm: "He has done it!" In any case, His complete surrender—
giving Himself into the power of a Roman governor, Roman tor-
turers, and Roman executioners, as well as committing Himself totally into the Father's hands (see Luke 23:46)—supplies the ultimate
example of what surrender looks like.

Surrendering Your Heart

The extent of Jesus's surrender was foreshadowed by Him when He
said, "No one takes [my life] from me, but I lay it down of my own
accord" (John 10:18). In His case, the act of surrender involved literally laying down His life. Our surrender may never come to that,
but it can feel like a death of sorts. When we surrender our will, our
preferences, our hearts, it can be a Gethsemane or Calvary experience, in which we must say, "Your will be done," or "You lay me in
the dust of death."

But the choice is ours. We can submit to the lies of the enemy
and forever strive to please the people around us—or we can submit
to God and His Word. We can surrender our hearts, wills, and lives
to the addiction, to people around us, to the will of our enemy, who
seeks to destroy us—or we can surrender to God.

Can you do that today? Can you take what you have—your
heart, your life, and your desire to please everyone around you in
every way, shape, or form—and surrender it all to God? Are you

able to picture what that looks like? You are placing your need to please everyone in God's hands. It's taking that youthful hope of being asked to sit at the cool kids' table and surrendering it to Him. It's laying down the need for the women in your church to seek you out to plan the next event, to lead a small group, to be invited on the women's retreat. It's laying down every desire to be invited to lunch by a friend, to be liked or complimented on Facebook, Instagram, or Twitter. It's telling God that He can have every dream that sets itself up in competition to another person, ministry, business, or organization. It's leaving the fear of rejection, failure, and isolation in the hands of the Almighty. It's deciding you will no longer be a victim of guilt and shame, or allowing the depression to consume you or define you. Numbers, names, titles—surrender it all to God. I know it's a lot. Surrender is hard. But there is blessing in obedience, as even Jesus modeled.

Look at Hebrews 5:7–9 with me:

During the days of Jesus' life on earth, he offered up prayers and petitions with fervent cries and tears to the one who could save him from death, and he was heard because of his reverent submission. Son though he was, he learned obedience from what he suffered and, once made perfect, he became the source of eternal salvation for all who obey him.

Did you catch that? It wasn't His Sonship that brought about His exaltation and ours; it was His "reverent submission." What a glorious truth.

And for us, as well, what an amazing exchange—to take all of our shame, fear, guilt, and pain, and place it into the big, rugged daddy hands of our heavenly Father, so that He can exchange it for freedom and blessing. Do you not long for that? That feeling of no longer being ashamed by those things you hide in your heart? Those painful pangs of jealousy and competition? Do you not long to know how it feels to be confident and fearless in your walk with the Lord, knowing that you are fully approved by Him?

Do this now with me. Take a piece of paper and draw a large heart on it. In it, write or draw everything that you struggle to surrender, whether they are the examples I mentioned above, or ones that have been stirring in your heart as you've been reading this book. Place every thought, idea, and name onto that heart. Then I want you to hold that heart in your hand and pray this with me:

> *Lord, this is my heart, my will, my life. I surrender it all to You, including those things that I have hidden in it—my secrets, my need to feel the approval of those around me. I place all of this, all of me, into Your hands. I release any control the enemy has had over this area of my life, as well as any control I have tried to exert. I ask You to change my desires from seeking the things I placed on this paper. From this day forward, I vow to seek Your approval and Yours alone. My heart, my will, and my life are all Yours for safekeeping. Do with me as You will. In Jesus's name, amen.*

Now, walk confidently and boldly, unashamed and without fear, into the claim and calling that God has on your life. Start today by digging into His Word and seeking Him to teach you about the authority and power you have in Him to continue finding deliverance from the cycle of addiction. Surrender your devices, your screen time, and your social media apps to Him daily, knowing that He has a better plan than the people who fill up the feed on your screens. This is how you will find freedom, daily, in your recovery, completely and totally surrendered to Him.

Lord, we surrender all to You—all that we think we are in exchange for what Your Word says we are. As approval addicts in recovery, we ask You to quicken Your Holy Spirit in us each day to surrender our thoughts, actions, and beliefs to You. We understand that we will stumble and sometimes fall, but we know You will always be there to pick us up. Be our Friend as we learn to be friends to those around us. Help us love others as You tell us to in Your Word, to love our neighbor as ourselves. That means without comparing, without jealousy, without overwhelming expectations, but in the same way that we want to be loved by others: in grace, humility, and compassion. It is only through You, the power of Your Word, and the work of the Holy Spirit in our lives that we can overcome and be healed from this addiction. We are placing our trust in You. In the mighty name of Jesus we pray, amen.

CONCLUSION

The End of Us Begins with You

• • • • • • • • • • •

How lucky I am to have something that
makes saying goodbye so hard.

WINNIE THE POOH

I hate goodbyes. I think that's why I'm usually the last one to leave a church event, a wedding, or a house party. It's even more of a struggle when I know it might be the last time I see you. It used to be a lot worse—I held on to friendships very tightly, especially those who poured into me, who loved me, and whom I loved back. When a sudden move or a loss of life removed one of those relationships from me, it felt like a rose being ripped through my hands.

Over time, however, I've learned better how to say goodbye. Years ago, a sweet friend said to me, "Dawn, people are going to constantly come and go in your life. You must learn to hold them with an open hand. God gives us friends but sometimes only for a season, and we have to learn how to let go." Ugh. Hearing those words was gut-wrenching to me, but I know they are true. Some people stay close our whole lives, but others we are given for a season. It's a rare treasure, at least for me, to hold my friends close for long periods of time.

And so it is, coming to the moment when we, too, must say goodbye. We've been on quite a journey together. I have worked hard to be honest, open, and completely vulnerable to you. As I have, I've pictured you every step of the way, sitting across from me, having coffee at our favorite coffee shop—the one with the big windows, the comfy chairs, and the smell of roasting espresso. We've come to know each other well, you and I. This season of journeying together, hearing each other's challenges, and sharing in one another's hurts has brought healing to me, and I hope it has to you as well.

I always pray, "God, knit our hearts together," over my friendships, and He has responded faithfully to that prayer. I feel like I am forever tethered to you. You have been faithful and have made it to the end. For that, I am eternally grateful.

You have changed me. Praying for you day after day, picturing you in your struggles and empathizing with your challenges, knowing that they were mine as well—it's brought me to a new place of humility, surrender, and trust in God. You have been on my heart since day one, and I promise that you will be there for many days to come, perhaps until my last breath. I am forever changed because of you.

I've thought long and hard about my final words to you. I feel as if I have been praying since the first time I realized this book needed to be written—maybe for you, maybe more so for me—about what I would say when it was all over. As the cursor on my computer screen blinks with anticipation, I wonder if I am capable of expressing the final words that lie so heavy on my heart, on this page.

They are words of encouragement, with a slight challenge added. As we sit together, with our lattes in front of us and my hand on yours, I know this may be the last time I get to speak these words into your life. I am looking deeply into your eyes. My heart is pounding with anticipation, my eyes are tearing up, and my voice—I know it is going to quiver a bit as I say these words to you.

I love you. Your friendship, your willingness to go to hard places with me and hear my stories has impacted me in a profound way. You have blessed me more than you may ever know or understand. But promise me this: Do not take what you have learned, all we have been through together, and keep it to yourself. I have poured out my heart to you, as a sacrificial offering to the Lord, not so that you could get spiritually fat on these words and keep them all for yourself. No, I did it so that you would be equipped to pass them on to another and another and another.

You have a sister, mother, coworker, or friend who is desperately drowning in a sea of approval addiction. She is afraid, she feels powerless, she is desperate and alone, and she needs you to give to her what you have received. She is like that girl in the beginning of this book—you. But now, you are powerful and confident.

You have seen God work miracles in your marriage and your relationships. You have closer friends, and you are no longer striving to make your home look like Pinterest. You've fasted from social media and have experienced how amazing it feels not to be tethered to your devices. You've experienced true freedom in understanding that your identity comes from God; you inherited it along with your salvation. You know now that God's approval is the only thing you need to live for; nothing else matters.

Now, woman of God, mighty warrior, daughter of the Most High King, take what you have been given and pour it all into that sister who is struggling now where you once were. Teach this to your children and model it for your friends. Show your spouse that you're so content in God's approval, he may never need to tell you that you look pretty again . . . okay, maybe that's taking it a bit too far . . .

This may be the end of our time together in the pages of this book, but really, it's just the beginning. I am passing the baton to you. This is now your story. Go out into this world and show them how far you have come. Hold your head high as a woman who walks in recovery, who knows who she is, and who is fully in love with her Savior for all He has done.

Father God, encourage our hearts today as we go our separate ways, knowing that our hearts are knitted together now, supernaturally, in You. Let Your will be done in our lives as Your children. Help us take what we have learned and share our newfound freedom in You with those around us. Don't let us keep it to ourselves. Keep us focused on You; help us remember that You are with us always. You'll never leave us or forsake us; instead, You empower us to share Your love with this lost and dying world. You have given us new eyes to see all the ways we can be free from the ongoing cycle of approval addiction. Remind us daily of Galatians 5:1, which says, "It is for freedom that Christ has set us free," so that as we encounter the temptation to seek the approval of others, we will choose freedom over bondage, knowing that we are already completely approved of by You. In Jesus's name, amen.

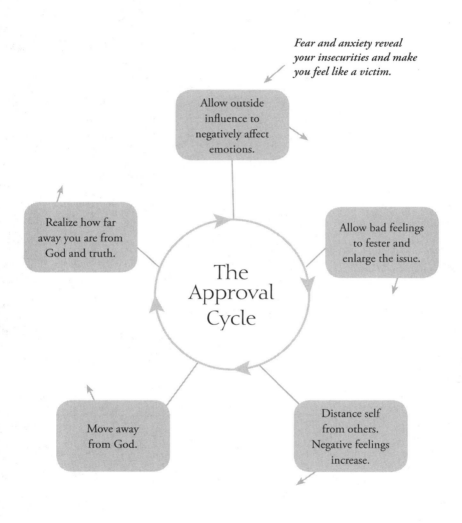

Fear and anxiety reveal your insecurities and make you feel like a victim.

Allow outside influence to negatively affect emotions.

Realize how far away you are from God and truth.

Allow bad feelings to fester and enlarge the issue.

The Approval Cycle

Move away from God.

Distance self from others. Negative feelings increase.

Like Me or Not

• • • • • • • • • •

OVERCOMING
APPROVAL ADDICTION

LEADER'S GUIDE

OVERCOMING APPROVAL ADDICTION AGREEMENT

This is a covenant agreement between me, _____,
my *Like Me or Not* group, and God, pledging that I am committed to the
journey of understanding how my need for people's approval has caused
challenges in my walk with the Lord and others. In recognizing my need to
further understand the identity that God has gifted me with, I commit to
the following:

- Reading the book *Like Me or Not* and accomplishing any other
  assigned materials for each week of the study.
- Being fully present at each meeting, putting away cell phones and
  other devices in order to engage with my group by listening to their
  struggles and celebrating their wins.
- Keeping the conversations of these meetings confidential, unless
  told otherwise by the member sharing—because one of the core
  issues of desiring people's approval is a need for trust and boundaries.
- Choosing to share what is on my heart and mind, as I feel God's
  leading, reminding myself that my approval comes from Him and
  not people. I recognize that other people's show of verbal and non-
  verbal approval will enable me through this process. Regardless, I
  will follow God's leading.
- Striving to be a living example of Ephesians 4:1–7 within this group
  in order to grow in the unity of the Spirit—by being humble,
  gentle, patient, and bearing with others in love.
- Being vulnerable enough to recognize those times I have become
  offended, jealous, or angry with another member. I will first pray
  about my heart and allow God to reveal the root issue when these
  feelings emerge. If I then feel the member sinned against me, I will
  use Matthew 18:15–17 as my model for reconciliation.

I agree to abide by this covenant to the best of my ability and to take it
seriously. I know that by signing this commitment I am submitting to the
Lord and the leadership of this group to seek healing, reconciliation, and redemption through my Lord Jesus Christ. I believe He can do immeasurably
more than we ask, seek, or imagine.

_____   _____
Signature   Date

INTRODUCTION

• • • • • • • • •

I am thrilled that you've decided to embark on a journey to understanding how your need for approval is prohibiting you from experiencing the full love of our heavenly Father. It's even more exciting to know that you want to do this in a small group or Sunday school class. I have written this Leader's Guide to accommodate an eight-week study.

Since there are sixteen chapters in the book, I have coupled them into two chapters for each week. Therefore, you will be prompted as to which chapters to read prior to the next week's questions. Each week you'll have questions to ask the class, but please be sure to start every session with prayer. God will lead you better than I ever could on this journey, and it is my hope that the Holy Spirit will be your guide through this process.

Should you need extra material, feel free to go through the chapters and pull in more material from them. You can always pull out the Scripture used in the chapters and do a deeper study on the verses to take your conversations a bit further.

Also, at the end of every chapter is a prayer. You can use those prayers to guide you as you prepare an ending prayer for each week.

Please know that I and others are praying for you in your role as leader of this study. If you are feeling the tug of the Holy Spirit to lead this class, then I believe you have been hand-selected by God to do so. If someone else steps forward from your circle of friends, don't step down. Instead, work together to colead the class. There's room for insight from both of you.

Perhaps you are feeling inadequate to lead because you feel so bound to approval addiction that you can barely see straight. Perfect. This is more opportunity for you to grow with others who will be feeling nearly the same way. God loves a humble and contrite spirit (Isaiah 66:2). He will honor you and bless you in your willingness to be obedient to Him.

So here is my commission to you as a chosen leader:

"You are a chosen people, a royal priesthood, a holy nation, God's special possession, that you may declare the praises of him who called you out of darkness into his wonderful light."[34]

You are a mighty warrior,[35] a minister of reconciliation,[36] created by God for a purpose. He knew in advance the calling that He would place on your life, and He is asking you to walk it out.[37]

Do not be afraid, the Lord is with you. He will fight for you; you only need to be still.[38] You are the apple of His eye,[39] knitted together in your mother's womb by His two hands.[40] Your identity is found in Him, and He deems it to be complete. Finished. You are not rising to this occasion because *you can*, but because *He can*, through you as a willing vessel. He will make up for every lack. If you lack wisdom, all you need to do is ask for it, and it will be yours.[41]

Go.

Love.

Serve.

And you will see God do immeasurably more than you ask or imagine.[42]

WEEK 1

Introduction
and *Reality Check*

• • • • • • • • •

Leader Prep for Week One: Prior to the first class, download and print off enough copies of the *Overcoming Approval Addiction Agreement* for each member of the class at dawnmowens.com/LikeMeorNot. For reference, a copy of the agreement can be found on page 186.

Day of the Class: Begin with a word of prayer, asking specifically for God to reveal Himself to the class according to their needs.

1. What was your favorite playtime activity as a child, and why did you love to participate in it?
2. In *Reality Check*, Dawn talks about her struggle with approval addiction. Were you able to relate to her struggle, and if so, how? If not, why not?
3. Do negative thoughts run through your mind about who you should be, could be, or ought to be? What are some of those thoughts, and how do they play into your need to seek approval from others?

4. In the *Introduction*, which individual can you relate to most—Kayla, Jessica, Tanya, or Rachel?

5. When you took the assessment, were there other questions you thought should be listed as indicators of having an addiction to approval? If so, what are they?

6. How does your need for approval play a role in your social media interactions?

7. How are you feeling about going on this journey? Excited? Nervous?

Leader: Distribute a copy of the *Overcoming Approval Addiction Agreement* to each class member. Ask someone to read it aloud while everyone else follows along. If they feel comfortable doing so, have each person sign their copy and return it to you. Hold on to these; you will return them to the participants in Week Eight.

End of class: Pray the Lord's Prayer located at the end of the *Introduction*.

Assignment: Remind the class to read *Puhlease, People* and *Me, Insecure?* Ask the class to review the questions in Week 2 prior to your time together, because it will be a bit lengthier than this week's class.

WEEK

2

Puhlease, People and *Me, Insecure?*

• • • • • • • • • •

Leader Prep for Week Two: This week's reading is a bit longer and meatier than Week One. If you think your time will run short, review the questions in advance and pick out the ones you know your class needs to discuss together.

Day of the Class: Begin by asking someone in the class to pray that God would reveal to each individual who they are in Him.

Repeat the Lord's Prayer located at the end of the *Introduction* on page 5.

1. Which do you relate to more—being a people-pleaser or being insecure? Or both? Why?
2. At what point in your life did your addiction to people-pleasing or insecurity manifest itself?
3. Have you ever felt like you lost who you were while trying to please other people?

Leader: Have the class self-identify who is extroverted (someone who is energized by being around other people) or an introvert (someone who gets their energy from alone time).

1. How does being an introvert or an extrovert affect how you seek approval from others?
2. Which one do you feel more like: Saul (who allowed his fear of what man thought to rule him and keep him from obeying God) or David (who knew he was a son of God and acted out that identity with courage and determination)?
3. How have you dealt in the past with people naming your insecurities in a public way? Did you get angry or depressed? Did you fight back or have some other reaction?
4. Could you relate to the approval addiction cycle highlighted in the middle of *Me, Insecure*? If so, how have you seen this played out in your life recently?
5. Can you see a correlation between the periods when you are spending time in God's Word and when you are not, how secure or insecure you feel about yourself?
6. Can you relate to Eve in second-guessing, "Did God *really* say that?"
7. In the future, how will you combat the enemy's lies about who you are? What can you do to remind yourself of who God says you are?

End of class: Remind the class to review the verses at the end of *Me, Insecure?* on page 50 (also located on page 211 of the *Appendix*) and start memorizing them if they have not already. Choose one scripture verse that you will memorize together for next week. End with a word of prayer focusing on how we don't have to perform to receive approval from God and how our confidence and security comes from Him.

Additional resources: *He Knows Who You Are* Scripture verses. Print it off at dawnmowens.com/LikeMeorNot.

Assignment: Read the next set of chapters: *My Way or the Highway* and *Don't Take it So Personally.* Memorize the verse selected from the end of *Me, Insecure?* on page 50 (also located on page 211 of the *Appendix*).

My Way or the Highway and *Don't Take It So Personally*

• • • • • • • • •

Leader Prep for Week Three: Make sure you have the verse you chose as a class memorized to go through together at the beginning of class.

Day of the Class: Choose someone to lead in prayer, asking God to reveal their need for control and to show them where they may have taken up offenses.

Repeat the scripture you memorized together.

1. Can you relate to Dawn when she confesses being a control freak? What situation are you struggling to control right now?
2. How does Job 1:21 speak to you in your current control situation?

3. What would it take for you to surrender that situation to the Lord?

4. Did you know approval addiction is a form of idolatry?

5. Do you think you will be able to change your focus in the future and not take up an offense when people speak against you in some way?

6. Dawn talks about three ways we will be tempted on page 74. Have you experienced these three temptations before? If so, how will you combat them in the future?

7. How can Exodus 14:14 help us overcome our need for control as we retrain our desire to be offended?

End of class: Pray through Ephesians 6 together, reminding the class that our battles are not against flesh and blood.

Assignment: Choose another Scripture verse from page 211 of the *Appendix* to memorize for next week.

WEEK

4

Community versus Comparison, That Chip on Your Shoulder, and Rejected!

• • • • • • • • •

Leader Prep for Week Four: Make sure you memorize the next Scripture verse from page 211 of the *Appendix* to repeat with the class this week. Prior to class, print off the *Pledge against Rejection* and the *Approval Addiction Cycle* from dawnmowens.com/LikeMeorNot.

Day of Class: Choose someone to pray for the class, asking God to reveal where they are comparing themselves with others and getting angry over things they need to respond to with love and grace.

Repeat the scripture you memorized together.

1. What does it mean to be a member of a community?
2. Do you prefer online community or offline?
3. How has your desire to compare and/or compete with others inhibited new or current relationships?

4. How can Paul's words in Ephesians 4:1–6 help us maintain the unity of the Spirit in the bond of peace, whether on- or offline?

5. Who have you held to impossibly high standards? How did you respond when you realized that person had failed to live up to your expectations?

6. Have you ever responded like Jonah did in Jonah 4:2–3, wanting God to bring His wrath on someone instead of extending grace and compassion?

7. How can you change your response to that person, realizing you don't have a good reason to be angry with them, according to what God has given to you?

8. Name a time when you had to overcome rejection for a larger cause.

9. *Rejected!* mentions a pledge to overcome the fear of rejection. What would it take for you to commit to the pledge? Once answered, hand out the *Pledge against Rejection* worksheets available on dawnmowens.com/LikeMeorNot. Read the pledge and then sign. Members can keep their own copies.

End of class: Pray through Jonah 4:2 together to remember how we are supposed to respond to each other in the likeness of our Creator. Repeat the Scripture verse from page 211 of the *Appendix* that you memorized for this week.

Assignment: Memorize Jonah 4:2 this week. Hand out the *Approval Addiction Cycle* chart printed from dawnmowens.com/LikeMeorNot. Ask members to work through the chapter as Dawn requested in a journal and using the *Approval Addiction Cycle* chart. Remind the class to read *One Day at a Time.*

WEEK

5

One Day at a Time

• • • • • • • • •

Leader Prep for Week Five: Memorize the next Scripture verse, Jonah 4:2, to repeat with the class this week. You will need to have filled out your *Approval Addiction Cycle* chart to use during class. You only have a few questions for this week; however, the third question will take up most of your time. The key to overcoming an addiction to approval is understanding the cycle and then learning how to break the cycle. **Do not skip question number three, as it is essential to equipping the class for the future.**

Day of Class: Choose someone to pray for the class this week, asking God to help them to make better choices, day by day. Ask someone to share the verse that they memorized with the class.

Repeat the scripture you memorized together.

1. Name a time when you were able to create a new positive habit to replace an old negative one.

2. On a scale of 1 to 5, with 5 being "I really want to overcome the addiction to seeking approval," and 1 being "it doesn't matter much to me," go around the class and ask everyone to rate where they are on the scale and why.

3. Take out the *Approval Addiction Cycle* chart (also on page 183). Ask each person to share a Scripture verse that they found to combat each area of the cycle. If that verse is helpful to you, add the Scripture reference to your chart so you can look it up later.

End of class: Pray to ask God to help each individual understand the cycle and then learn how to overcome it through His Word.

Assignment: Have each class member choose a verse they identified on the *Approval Addiction Cycle* chart during class. Ask them to share their verse selection with the class and then memorize it for week six. Read *Know Who You Are* and *Obsession (Not the Perfume)*.

Know Who You Are and Obsession (Not the Perfume)

• • • • • • • • •

Leader Prep for Week Six: Make sure you have your verse memorized for this week.

Day of Class: Choose someone to pray for the class this week, asking God to affirm their identity in Him. Ask someone to share the verse they memorized last week with the class and tell how it was helpful.

1. Have you ever felt like a failure? How did it cause you to respond to the situation you were in?
2. Did you actually fail in that situation, or did you later realize you had fabricated the problem in your mind?
3. Identify one thing the Lord has redeemed in your life and share it with the class.
4. Before you read the chapter *Know Who You Are,* did you understand that redemption is part of God's salvation process?

5. Have you ever thought of your identity as part of your redemption in Christ? How does this idea help you to understand who you are and how you are to live?

6. What does it mean to live your life sacrificially, transforming your mind and not conforming to this world?

End of Class: Ask if anyone became a new believer or rededicated their life to Christ through the reading this week. Ask them to share their testimony on the *Testimony* form on dawnmowens.com/LikeMeorNot. Pray that God would make Romans 12:1–2 real to each person as they go through this next week.

Assignment: Memorize Romans 12:1–2 for next week's class. As you memorize, ask the Lord to show you ways you can live sacrificially in order not to conform to this world. Write them down to share with the class next week. Read *Peace Junkie* and *A Joy-a-holic*.

7

Peace Junkie and A Joy-a-holic

• • • • • • • • • •

Leader Prep for Week Seven: Be sure to have Romans 12:1–2 memorized for this week. Be prepared to talk about the things that the Lord showed you to steer clear of in conforming to this world.

Day of Class: Choose someone to pray for the class this week, asking God to teach them how to pursue peace and choose joy daily. Ask someone to share what they learned this past week while memorizing Romans 12:1–2.

Repeat the scripture you memorized together.

1. Explain what you think peace and joy look like in everyday life.
2. Do you believe you can experience peace and joy, even in the midst of trials and suffering? If so, share an example. If not, explain why you think it is impossible.

3. Name something you crave, whether it's a food, a TV show, a person, or an experience.

4. Read three different versions, including the Amplified Version, of Psalm 34:14. Which version do you prefer as it pertains to peace, and why?

5. What do you think it might look like for you to crave peace, and how would you make that possible every day?

6. Read James 1:2–4. What sounds odd about these verses? Why do you think James makes such a bold statement at the beginning of his letter?

7. Have you ever been in a situation where things were not going your way and you were complaining to everyone, including God?

8. How different would it be for you to choose joy over those challenging circumstances than whatever your attitude has been?

9. Which area do you need to focus on first—seeking peace or choosing joy?

End of class: Ask someone to close the class in prayer, specifically addressing the issues people in the class have brought up. Ask God to help each class member to crave peace and choose joy.

Assignment: Remind the class to read *The Surrender Habit* and *The End of Us Begins with You*. Each person should choose which area they struggle with more: peace or joy. Then memorize the Amplified version of Psalm 34:14, which says, "Depart from evil and do good; seek, inquire for, and crave peace and pursue (go after) it" (AMPC) or James 1:2–4.

WEEK 8

The Surrender Habit and *The End of Us Begins with You*

• • • • • • • • •

Leader Prep for Week Eight: Be sure to have one of the verses memorized from Week Seven. You may want to have snacks or something to celebrate the ending of the class with participants. Locate the *Overcoming Approval Addiction Agreement* from Week One to return to class members today.

Day of Class: Choose someone to pray for the class this week, focusing on asking God to teach them how to surrender and take the next steps necessary after this class. Ask someone to share what they learned this past week while memorizing their verse.

Repeat the scripture you memorized together.

> 1. What does the word *surrender* mean to you? Does it have a positive or negative connotation? Why?

2. On a scale of 1 to 10 (one being easy, ten being very hard), how difficult do you think it is to surrender on a regular basis?

3. How did you feel about Dawn's comparison of surrendering an approval addiction to a drug or alcohol addiction? Do you think they are similar or different? Is it easier or harder to overcome approval addiction compared to other addictions?

4. Does it give you peace to know that your Savior also came to a place of surrender in the garden of Gethsemane?

5. Read Psalm 22 together. What does this verse say about the necessity to surrender our need for approval and seek God instead?

6. Reflect back on who you were when you started this study. When you are ready, share one significant lesson you have learned during our journey together.

7. What will you do with what you have learned? How will you maintain your recovery from here? Whom will you ask to join you in your journey?

8. Hand out the *Overcoming Approval Addiction Agreements* from the first class. Have someone read the agreement out loud. What thoughts do you have on the agreement, now that you have completed the class? What will you do with the agreement after class is through?

9. As our last act together, pair up in groups of two or three. Take a moment to pray for each other. During the prayer time, ask the Lord to do immeasurably more than each person can ask or imagine in setting them free from the addiction of approval, so they will know that their identity is complete in Him.

A SPECIAL NOTE

• • • • • • • • •

Thank you for taking this journey with me. Together, we've learned to seek God daily to overcome the addiction to approval. It is my prayer, as we come to the end of this class, that you know more of who you are and whose you are. There's no further need to worry about what others think of you. You can rest in knowing you are complete and satisfied in Him.

If you need more encouragement or inspiration, check out my website at dawnmowens.com or follow me on Facebook at Dawn Marie Owens, on Twitter as @dawnmarieowens, and on Instagram as @dawn.m.owens.

I would love to hear from you. If you have a testimony or feedback about the book or the Leader's Guide, or if you want me to consider other ways to help people overcome the addiction to approval, please do not hesitate to email me at dawnowens@linkingcullman.org.

Dawn M Owens

Appendix

• • • • • • • • • • •

Here are Bible verses that have helped me with my approval addiction. Look them up in your favorite version, or try different versions to get a new perspective.

Identity

1 Corinthians 6:20

Ephesians 3:11

1 Samuel 13:14

Genesis 1:27

Isaiah 61:7

Galatians 3:26

Romans 8:17

1 Peter 2:9

Ephesians 2:10

John 15:15

Isaiah 61:3

Ephesians 4:1–6

Micah 6:8

Psalm 139:13

2 Corinthians 5:17

Ephesians 2:6

Psalm 17:8

Zephaniah 3:17

Surrender

Matthew 6:9–13

Job 1:21

Matthew 26:42

Luke 23:46

John 10:18

1 Samuel 17:37

Jonah 4:2–3

Exodus 14:14

People-Pleasing

1 Samuel 15:24

Galatians 1:10

John 12:42–43

1 Thessalonians 2:4

Forgiveness

Colossians 3:13

Lamentations 3:22–23

2 Corinthians 2:11

Insecurity

Genesis 3:1

Fear/Anxiety/Worry

2 Timothy 1:7

Philippians 4:6–7

Philippians 4:11

Jonah 4:4

Romans 8:28

Proverbs 29:25

Psalm 34:4

Renewing Your Mind

Romans 12:1–2

Luke 10:27

Psalm 34:14

Spiritual Attack

John 10:10

Ephesians 6:12–17

Revelation 12:11

James 4:7

Isaiah 54:7

Facing Temptation

Romans 7:18

Galatians 5:1

Suffering

James 1:2–4

Romans 5:3

Psalm 22:22–24

Hebrews 5:7–9

MEMORIZATION SCRIPTURES

• • • • • • • • •

But you are a chosen people, a royal priesthood,
a holy nation, God's special possession,
that you may declare the praises of him
who called you out of darkness into his wonderful light.
1 Peter 2:9

For we are God's masterpiece.
He has created us anew in Christ Jesus,
so we can do the good things
he planned for us long ago.
Ephesians 2:10 NLT

For in Christ Jesus you are all
sons (daughters) of God, through faith.
Galatians 3:26 ESV

No longer do I call you servants,
for the servant does not know what his master is doing;
but I have called you friends,
for all that I have heard from my Father
I have made known to you.
John 15:15 ESV

From the Bottom of My Heart

This book exists because of the prayers of so many. To Bob, Robin, Julie, Cheryl, Anna, Elissa, Jillian, Tara, and Sara—your prayers kept me going every step of the way. You have my deepest gratitude.

Julie G., your dedication to editing the entire manuscript will always be a gift to me. Leslie, Paige, and Clancy, you put up with my chapter review requests and external processing needs, thank you for your time and patience.

To my agents at *Hartline*, Cyle and Tessa, you gave this newbie a chance to bring a God-dream to life, thanks for all you do to support this book.

To the team at *Worthy Publishing*—Jeana, Marilyn, Rachel, Cat, and Nicole—you have blown me away with your wisdom and experience. You are dream-makers and I am forever grateful that God allowed me to serve in ministry with you during this time.

To my enablers at The Link of Cullman County, your belief in a vision larger than me and commitment to the kingdom of God inspires me daily. You have my heart always.

Mom and Kim, you have always been my biggest cheerleaders. May the words on these pages minister from my heart to yours. I carry your heart with me . . .

Sawyer, this message, my son, is my prayer for you. God knows you and loves you, even more than me and Daddy. Seek to know Him and all else will come.

Chris, your prayers, support, and love have poured into the pages of this book. Thank you for believing in me before I could see it in myself.

This is my sacrificial love offering to you, Daddy. May it please you and give you glory in every way.

Notes

• • • • • • • • • •

1. Steven Gledhill, founder, author, and editor of FREEdom from MEdom Project. http://www.freedomfrommedom.com/wp3/founder-author-editor.

2. Matthew 6:9–13 KJV.

3. "Overcome," Dictionary.com, accessed August 11, 2016, http://www.dictionary.com/browse/overcome?s=t.

4. Carol Bainbridge. "The Truth about Introverts and Their Needs." Verywell. June 11, 2017. Accessed June 30, 2017. https://www.verywell.com/all-about-introverts-1449354.

5. National Institute on Drug Abuse. "Preface." NIDA. Accessed June 19, 2017. https://www.drugabuse.gov/publications/drugs-brains-behavior-science-addiction.

6. Gwenn Schurgin O'Keeffe, Kathleen Clarke-Pearson, and Council on Communications and Media. "Clinical Report: The Impact of Social Media on Children, Adolescents, and Families." *Pediatrics*. March 22, 2011. Accessed January 2, 2017. http://pediatrics.aappublications.org/content/early/2011/03/28/peds.2011-0054.

7. Damon Beres. "5 Weird Negative Effects of Social Media on Your Brain | Reader's Digest." *Reader's Digest*. February 08, 2017. Accessed June 30, 2017. http://www.rd.com/health/wellness/negative-effects-of-social-media/4/.

8. Joseph Nowinski. *The Tender Heart: Conquering Your Insecurity*. New York: Simon & Schuster, 2001.

9. Galatians 3:26.

10. Romans 8:17.

11. 1 Peter 2:9.

12. Ephesians 2:10.

13. Isaiah 61:3.

14. Bob Hostetler. *American Idols: The Worship of the American Dream*. Nashville, TN: Broadman & Holman Publishers, 2006, p. 5.

15. "Focus." Merriam-Webster. Accessed June 9, 2017. https://www.merriam-webster.com/dictionary/focus.

16. The Boundaries Books Team. "How to Overcome a Victim Mentality." Boundaries Books. September 19, 2016. Accessed February 3, 2017. http://www.boundariesbooks.com/boundaries-with-kids/overcome-victim-mentality/.

17. "Jesus Is Tempted to Abandon Serving God (Luke 4:1–13)." Jesus Is Tempted to Abandon Serving God (Luke 4:1–13)—Theology of Work. Accessed February 6, 2017. https://www.theologyofwork.org/new-testament/luke/the-kingdom-of-god-shows-up-at-work-luke/jesus-is-tempted-to-abandon-serving-god.

18. "Why Did Mark Zuckerberg Create Facebook?" Zimbio. Accessed March 10, 2017. http://www.zimbio.com/Why Did Mark Zuckerberg Create Facebook/articles/irW6fWzojv2/Mark Zuckerberg Create Facebook.

19. "Community." Merriam-Webster.com. Accessed July 3, 2017. https://www.merriam
-webster.com/dictionary/community.
20. "Compassion." Dictionary.com. Accessed March 21, 2017. http://www.dictionary.com
/browse/compassion.
21. Spiros Zodhiates. *Hebrew-Greek Key Word Study Bible: Key Insights into God's Word:
NASB, New American Standard Bible.* Chattanooga, TN: AMG Publishers, 2008,
p. 1870.
22. Zodhiates, 1952.
23. Sam Laird. "Cyberbullying: Scourge of the Internet [INFOGRAPHIC]." Mashable.
July 08, 2012. Accessed July 12, 2017. http://mashable.com/2012/07/08/
cyberbullying-infographic/#iy0L4AXJYaq7.
24. "Cultivate What Matters." Cultivate What Matters RSS. Accessed July 12, 2017.
http://www.cultivatewhatmatters.com.
25. Larry Scheikart and Michael Allen. *A Patriot's History of the United States.* New York,
NY: Penguin Group, 2004, p. 667.
26. Ibid.
27. Spiro Zodhiates, "James." *Key Word Study Bible*, edited by Warren Baker and Joel
Kletzing. Chattanooga, TN: AMG Publishers, 2008, p. 1636.
28. Wikipedia. July 11, 2017. Accessed May 18, 2017. https://en.wikipedia.org/wiki
/Twelve-step_program.
29. Ibid.
30. Wikipedia. July 11, 2017. Accessed May 18, 2017. https://en.wikipedia.org/wiki
/Twelve-step_program.
31. Ibid.
32. "Surrender." Merriam-Webster.com. Accessed July 12, 2017. https://www.merriam
-webster.com/dictionary/surrender.
33. Psalm 22:3–4, 14–15,19, 31.
34. 1 Peter 2:9.
35. Zephaniah 3:17.
36. 2 Corinthians 5:18.
37. Ephesians 2:10.
38. Exodus 14:14.
39. Zechariah 2:8.
40. Psalm 139:13.
41. James 1:5.
42. Ephesians 3:20.

About the Author

● ● ● ● ● ● ● ● ●

Dawn fell in love with reading books and writing as a child. After receiving Christ as her Savior at age twenty-six, God rocked her world. She committed every talent she had to Him. Now, as the founder/ executive director of the Link of Cullman County, in Cullman, Alabama, and as an award-winning author, Dawn shares her talents for writing, speaking, and loving people by ministering to the poor, the hopeless, the addicted, and the broken. You can learn more about The Link of Cullman County at linkingcullman.org. Dawn is donating her proceeds from the sale of *Like Me or Not* to continue the Link of Cullman County's ministry efforts.

She likes to blog about inspiring others to seek God and His glory at dawnmowens.com. She is a wife, mom, and friend to anyone who loves lattes in coffeehouses.

IF YOU ENJOYED THIS BOOK, WILL YOU CONSIDER SHARING THE MESSAGE WITH OTHERS?

Mention the book in a blog post or through Facebook, Twitter, Pinterest, or upload a picture through Instagram.

Recommend this book to those in your small group, book club, workplace, and classes.

Head over to facebook.com/dawnmowensauthor, "LIKE" the page, and post a comment as to what you enjoyed the most.

Tweet "I recommend reading #LikeMeOrNot by @dawnmarieowens // @worthypub"

Pick up a copy for someone you know who would be challenged and encouraged by this message.

Write a book review online.